REGIONAL AND STATE EMPLOYMENT AND UNEMPLOYMENT — JANUARY 2015

Regional and state unemployment rates were little changed in January. Twenty-four states had unemployment rate decreases from December, 8 states had increases, and 18 states and the District of Columbia had no change, the U.S. Bureau of Labor Statistics reported today. Forty-five states and the District of Columbia had unemployment rate decreases from a year earlier, three states had increases, and two states had no change. The national jobless rate was little changed from December at 5.7 percent but was 0.9 percentage point lower than in January 2014.

In January 2015, nonfarm payroll employment increased in 39 states, decreased in 10 states and the District of Columbia, and was unchanged in North Carolina. The largest over-the-month increases in employment occurred in California (+67,300), Ohio (+25,100), and Michigan (+24,200). The largest over-the-month decrease in employment occurred in Virginia (-10,900), followed by Minnesota (-7,900) and Louisiana (-7,500). The largest over-the-month percentage increase in employment occurred in Idaho (+1.4 percent), followed by Hawaii (+0.9 percent) and Utah (+0.7 percent). The largest over-the-month percentage decline in employment occurred in Maine (-0.6 percent), followed by Louisiana and New Hampshire (-0.4 percent each). Over the year, nonfarm employment increased in 49 states and the District of Columbia and decreased in Maine (-0.1 percent). The largest over-the-year percentage increase occurred in North Dakota (+4.3 percent), followed by Utah (+4.0 percent) and Florida and Nevada (+3.6 percent each).

Regional, State, and Metropolitan Area Data Series Changes

In accordance with standard practices, historical data have been revised in tables 1 through 6 of this news release. For detailed information on changes to the data, see the box notes at the end of the news release.

Regional Unemployment (Seasonally Adjusted)

In January, the Midwest had the lowest regional unemployment rate, 5.2 percent, while the West had the highest rate, 6.3 percent. Over the month, only the South had a statistically significant unemployment rate change (-0.1 percentage point). Significant over-the-year rate decreases occurred in all four regions: the Midwest (-1.4 percentage points), Northeast (-1.1 points), West (-1.0 point), and South (-0.9 point). (See table 1.)

Among the nine geographic divisions, the West North Central had the lowest unemployment rate, 4.2 percent in January. The Pacific had the highest rate, 6.7 percent. Over the month, no division had a statistically significant change in its jobless rate. All nine divisions had significant rate declines from a year earlier, with the largest of these decreases occurring in the East North Central (-1.6 percentage points). The next largest over-the-year unemployment rate decreases were in the Middle Atlantic, Mountain, and New England divisions (-1.1 percentage points each).

State Unemployment (Seasonally Adjusted)

North Dakota had the lowest jobless rate in January, 2.8 percent. Mississippi and Nevada had the highest unemployment rates among the states, 7.1 percent each. The District of Columbia had a rate of 7.7 percent. In total, 21 states had unemployment rates significantly lower than the U.S. figure of 5.7 percent, 10 states and the District of Columbia had measurably higher rates, and 19 states had rates that were not appreciably different from that of the nation. (See tables A and 3 and chart 1.)

In January, nine states had statistically significant over-the-month unemployment rate changes, all of which were declines. Oregon had the largest rate decrease (-0.4 percentage point), followed by Idaho, Maine, and Rhode Island (-0.3 point each). The remaining 41 states and the District of Columbia had jobless rates that were not measurably different from those of a month earlier, though some had changes that were at least as large numerically as the significant changes. (See table B.)

Forty-two states had statistically significant unemployment rate declines from January 2014, the largest of which occurred in Illinois and Rhode Island (-2.1 percentage points each). The only significant over-the-year rate increases occurred in Louisiana (+1.5 percentage points) and South Carolina (+0.3 point). The remaining six states and the District of Columbia had rates that were not appreciably different from those of a year earlier. (See table C.)

Nonfarm Payroll Employment (Seasonally Adjusted)

In January 2015, 18 states had statistically significant over-the-month changes in employment, 15 of which were increases. The largest significant job gains occurred in California (+67,300), Ohio (+25,100), and Michigan (+24,200). The three significant decreases occurred in Virginia (-10,900), Louisiana (-7,500), and Maine (-3,400). (See tables D and 5.)

Over the year, 38 states and the District of Columbia had statistically significant changes in employment, all of which were positive. The largest significant over-the-year job increase occurred in California (+498,000), followed by Texas (+392,900) and Florida (+274,100). (See table E and chart 2.)

———————

The Metropolitan Area Employment and Unemployment news release for January 2015 is scheduled to be released on Friday, March 20, 2015, at 10:00 a.m. (EDT). The Regional and State Employment and Unemployment news release for February 2015 is scheduled to be released on Friday, March 27, 2015, at 10:00 a.m. (EDT).

Changes to Local Area Unemployment Statistics Data

Effective with the release of Regional and State Unemployment 2014 Annual Averages on March 4, 2015, the civilian labor force and unemployment data for regions, divisions, states, the District of Columbia, and the modeled substate areas presented in tables 1-4 of this news release were replaced with data produced using a new generation of time-series models. Data were re-estimated back to January 1976 for regions, divisions, states, the District of Columbia, the Los Angeles-Long Beach-Glendale metropolitan division, New York City, and the balances of California and New York states. Data for the five remaining modeled substate and balance-of-state areas were re-estimated back to their new series beginnings in 1990 or 1994. Both seasonally adjusted and not seasonally adjusted data were affected. More information is available in the "Report on Revision to State and Area Time-Series Models" on the BLS website at www.bls.gov/lau/lauschanges2015.htm.

The revisions to model-based data at the state level and below for 2013 and 2014 also incorporated updated estimation inputs, while the revisions for all model-based data from April 2010 forward reflected new population controls from the U.S. Census Bureau.

Changes to Current Employment Statistics Data

Effective with this release, nonfarm payroll estimates for states and metropolitan areas have been revised as a result of annual benchmark processing to reflect 2014 employment counts primarily from the BLS Quarterly Census of Employment and Wages (QCEW) (tables 5 and 6), as well as updated seasonal adjustment factors. Not seasonally adjusted data beginning with April 2013 and seasonally adjusted data beginning with January 2010 were subject to revision. Some seasonally adjusted series may have been revised back to 1990. For more information on annual processing see www.bls.gov/sae/benchmark2015.pdf.

Table A. States with unemployment rates significantly different from that of the U.S., January 2015, seasonally adjusted

State	Rate [p]
United States [1]	5.7
Arizona	6.6
California	6.9
Colorado	4.2
Delaware	5.0
District of Columbia	7.7
Georgia	6.4
Hawaii	4.1
Idaho	4.1
Iowa	4.2
Kansas	4.2
Louisiana	7.0
Minnesota	3.7
Mississippi	7.1
Montana	4.4
Nebraska	2.9
Nevada	7.1
New Hampshire	4.0
North Dakota	2.8
Ohio	5.1
Oklahoma	3.9
Pennsylvania	5.1
Rhode Island	6.5
South Carolina	6.6
South Dakota	3.4
Tennessee	6.7
Texas	4.4
Utah	3.4
Vermont	4.1
Virginia	4.7
Washington	6.4
Wisconsin	5.0
Wyoming	4.0

[1] Data are not preliminary.

[p] = preliminary.

Table B. States with statistically significant unemployment rate changes from December 2014 to January 2015, seasonally adjusted

State	Rate		Over-the-month change [p]
	December 2014	January 2015 [p]	
California	7.1	6.9	-0.2
Idaho	4.4	4.1	-.3
Iowa	4.3	4.2	-.1
Maine	5.5	5.2	-.3
Massachusetts	5.3	5.1	-.2
Nebraska	3.1	2.9	-.2
Oregon	6.7	6.3	-.4
Rhode Island	6.8	6.5	-.3
Wyoming	4.2	4.0	-.2

[p] = preliminary.

Table C. States with statistically significant unemployment rate changes from January 2014 to January 2015, seasonally adjusted

State	Rate		Over-the-year change [p]
	January 2014	January 2015 [p]	
Alabama	7.2	6.0	-1.2
Alaska	6.9	6.3	-.6
Arizona	7.1	6.6	-.5
Arkansas	6.6	5.6	-1.0
California	8.1	6.9	-1.2
Colorado	5.8	4.2	-1.6
Connecticut	7.1	6.3	-.8
Delaware	6.1	5.0	-1.1
Florida	6.5	5.7	-.8
Georgia	7.3	6.4	-.9
Hawaii	4.7	4.1	-.6
Idaho	5.1	4.1	-1.0
Illinois	8.2	6.1	-2.1
Iowa	4.4	4.2	-.2
Kansas	4.7	4.2	-.5
Kentucky	7.5	5.5	-2.0
Louisiana	5.5	7.0	1.5
Maine	6.0	5.2	-.8
Maryland	6.0	5.5	-.5
Massachusetts	6.1	5.1	-1.0
Michigan	7.9	6.3	-1.6
Minnesota	4.5	3.7	-.8
Mississippi	7.9	7.1	-.8
Missouri	6.4	5.5	-.9
Montana	5.0	4.4	-.6
Nebraska	3.5	2.9	-.6
Nevada	8.5	7.1	-1.4
New Hampshire	4.6	4.0	-.6
New Jersey	7.1	6.3	-.8
New Mexico	6.7	5.9	-.8
New York	6.8	5.8	-1.0
North Carolina	6.6	5.4	-1.2
Ohio	6.5	5.1	-1.4
Oklahoma	5.0	3.9	-1.1
Oregon	7.2	6.3	-.9
Pennsylvania	6.3	5.1	-1.2
Rhode Island	8.6	6.5	-2.1
South Carolina	6.3	6.6	.3
Texas	5.5	4.4	-1.1
Utah	3.9	3.4	-.5
Virginia	5.3	4.7	-.6
West Virginia	6.8	5.9	-.9
Wisconsin	6.0	5.0	-1.0
Wyoming	4.3	4.0	-.3

[p] = preliminary.

Table D. States with statistically significant employment changes from December 2014 to January 2015, seasonally adjusted

State	December 2014	January 2015 [p]	Over-the-month change [p]
California	15,860,700	15,928,000	67,300
Connecticut	1,678,100	1,684,500	6,400
Hawaii	626,000	631,500	5,500
Idaho	659,100	668,400	9,300
Louisiana	1,996,600	1,989,100	-7,500
Maine	604,700	601,300	-3,400
Michigan	4,217,600	4,241,800	24,200
Mississippi	1,124,500	1,129,100	4,600
Missouri	2,744,600	2,758,900	14,300
Nebraska	996,800	1,001,500	4,700
Nevada	1,230,500	1,237,200	6,700
New Jersey	3,982,300	3,994,700	12,400
Ohio	5,369,900	5,395,000	25,100
Oregon	1,745,400	1,753,000	7,600
Tennessee	2,850,900	2,859,200	8,300
Utah	1,353,600	1,363,300	9,700
Virginia	3,797,300	3,786,400	-10,900
Washington	3,122,600	3,140,900	18,300

[p] = preliminary.

Table E. States with statistically significant employment changes from January 2014 to January 2015, seasonally adjusted

State	January 2014	January 2015 [p]	Over-the-year change [p]
Alabama	1,910,300	1,945,200	34,900
Arizona	2,546,200	2,614,200	68,000
Arkansas	1,179,800	1,206,600	26,800
California	15,430,000	15,928,000	498,000
Colorado	2,425,400	2,496,500	71,100
Connecticut	1,659,900	1,684,500	24,600
Delaware	435,600	442,500	6,900
District of Columbia	748,100	760,200	12,100
Florida	7,705,500	7,979,600	274,100
Georgia	4,090,200	4,222,100	131,900
Idaho	648,200	668,400	20,200
Illinois	5,834,900	5,899,900	65,000
Indiana	2,951,900	3,017,600	65,700
Iowa	1,537,400	1,562,200	24,800
Kansas	1,382,000	1,399,300	17,300
Kentucky	1,843,700	1,883,900	40,200
Louisiana	1,964,400	1,989,100	24,700
Maryland	2,603,000	2,641,800	38,800
Massachusetts	3,380,500	3,448,500	68,000
Michigan	4,143,500	4,241,800	98,300
Minnesota	2,795,200	2,823,500	28,300
Missouri	2,715,700	2,758,900	43,200
Nebraska	989,300	1,001,500	12,200
Nevada	1,193,800	1,237,200	43,400
New Jersey	3,945,600	3,994,700	49,100
New Mexico	816,000	828,900	12,900
New York	9,008,600	9,166,300	157,700
North Carolina	4,095,400	4,203,100	107,700
North Dakota	451,000	470,500	19,500
Ohio	5,297,200	5,395,000	97,800
Oklahoma	1,644,700	1,669,400	24,700
Oregon	1,697,400	1,753,000	55,600
Pennsylvania	5,759,600	5,822,000	62,400
South Carolina	1,928,200	1,979,400	51,200
Tennessee	2,787,500	2,859,200	71,700
Texas	11,376,700	11,769,600	392,900
Utah	1,310,700	1,363,300	52,600
Washington	3,040,800	3,140,900	100,100
Wisconsin	2,829,300	2,872,600	43,300

[p] = preliminary.

Technical Note

This release presents labor force and unemployment data for census regions and divisions, states, and selected substate areas from the Local Area Unemployment Statistics (LAUS) program (tables 1 to 4). Also presented are nonfarm payroll employment estimates by state and industry supersector from the Current Employment Statistics (CES) program (tables 5 and 6). The LAUS and CES programs are both federal-state cooperative endeavors.

Labor force and unemployment—from the LAUS program

Definitions. The labor force and unemployment data are based on the same concepts and definitions as those used for the official national estimates obtained from the Current Population Survey (CPS), a sample survey of households that is conducted for the Bureau of Labor Statistics (BLS) by the U.S. Census Bureau. The LAUS program measures employment and unemployment on a place-of-residence basis. The universe for each is the civilian noninstitutional population 16 years of age and over. Employed persons are those who did any work at all for pay or profit in the reference week (the week including the 12th of the month) or worked 15 hours or more without pay in a family business or farm, plus those not working who had a job from which they were temporarily absent, whether or not paid, for such reasons as bad weather, labor-management dispute, illness, or vacation. Unemployed persons are those who were not employed during the reference week (based on the definition above), had actively looked for a job sometime in the 4-week period ending with the reference week, and were currently available for work; persons on layoff expecting recall need not be looking for work to be counted as unemployed. The labor force is the sum of employed and unemployed persons. The unemployment rate is the number of unemployed as a percent of the labor force.

Method of estimation. Estimates for 48 of the 50 states, the District of Columbia, the Los Angeles-Long Beach-Glendale metropolitan division, New York City, and the balances of California and New York State are produced using time-series models. This method, which underwent substantial enhancement at the beginning of 2015, utilizes data from several sources, including the CPS, the CES, and state unemployment insurance (UI) programs. Estimates for the state of California are derived by summing the estimates for the Los Angeles-Long Beach-Glendale metropolitan division and the balance of California. Similarly, estimates for New York State are derived by summing the estimates for New York City and the balance of New York State. Estimates for the nine census divisions, as well as the five additional substate areas contained in this release (the Cleveland-Elyria and Detroit-Warren-Dearborn metropolitan areas and the Chicago-Naperville-Arlington Heights, Miami-Miami Beach-Kendall, and Seattle-Bellevue-Everett metropolitan divisions) and their respective balances of state are based on similar model-based approaches. Estimates for census regions are obtained by summing the model-based estimates for the component divisions. Each month, census division estimates are controlled to the national totals; state estimates are then controlled to their respective division totals. Substate and balance-of-state estimates for the five areas noted above are controlled to their respective state totals. Estimates for Puerto Rico are derived from a monthly household survey similar to the CPS. A detailed description of the estimation procedures is available from BLS upon request.

Annual revisions. Labor force and unemployment data for prior years reflect adjustments made at the end of each year. The adjusted estimates reflect updated population data from the U.S. Census Bureau, any revisions in the other data sources, and model re-estimation. In most years, historical data for the most recent five years (both seasonally adjusted and not seasonally adjusted) are revised near the beginning of each calendar year, prior to the release of January estimates. With the introduction of a new generation of times-series models in early 2015, historical data were re-estimated back to the series beginnings in 1976, 1990, or 1994.

Seasonal adjustment. The LAUS program introduced smoothed seasonally adjusted (SSA) estimates in January 2010. These are seasonally adjusted data that have incorporated a long-run trend smoothing procedure, resulting in estimates that are less volatile than those previously produced. The estimates are smoothed using a Henderson Trend Filter (H13). The H13 uses a filtering procedure, based on moving averages, to remove the irregular fluctuations from the seasonally adjusted series, leaving the trend. The same process is used on both historical and current year estimates. For more information about the smoothing technique, see the BLS website at www.bls.gov/lau/lassaqa.htm.

Area definitions. The substate area data published in this release reflect the delineations issued by the U.S. Office of Management and Budget on February 28, 2013. A detailed list of the geographic definitions is available online at www.bls.gov/lau/lausmsa.htm.

Employment—from the CES program

Definitions. Employment data refer to persons on establishment payrolls who receive pay for any part of the pay period that includes the 12th of the month. Persons are counted at their place of work rather than at their place of residence; those appearing on more than one payroll are counted on each payroll. Industries are classified on the basis of their principal activity in accordance with the 2012 version of the North American Industry Classification System.

Method of estimation. CES State and Area employment data are produced using several estimation procedures. Where possible these data are produced using a "weighted link relative" estimation technique in which a ratio of current month weighted employment to that of the previous-month weighted employment is computed from a sample of establishments reporting for both months. The estimates of employment for the current month are then obtained by multiplying these ratios by the previous month's employment estimates. The weighted link relative technique is utilized for data series where the sample size meets certain statistical criteria.

For some employment series, the sample of establishments is very small or highly variable. In these cases, a model-based approach is used in estimation. These models use the direct sample estimates (described above), combined with forecasts of historical (benchmarked) data to decrease volatility in estimation. Two different models (Fay-Herriot Model and Small Domain Model) are used depending on the industry level being estimated. For more detailed information about each model, refer to the BLS Handbook of Methods.

Annual revisions. Employment estimates are adjusted annually to a complete count of jobs, called benchmarks, derived principally from tax reports that are submitted by employers who are covered under state unemployment insurance (UI) laws. The benchmark information is used to adjust the monthly estimates between the new benchmark and the preceding one and also to establish the level of employment for the new benchmark month. Thus, the benchmarking process establishes the level of employment, and the sample is used to measure the month-to-month changes in the level for the subsequent months.

Seasonal adjustment. Payroll employment data are seasonally adjusted at the statewide supersector level. In some states, the seasonally adjusted payroll employment total is computed by aggregating the independently adjusted supersector series. In other states, the seasonally adjusted payroll employment total is independently adjusted. Revisions of historical data for the most recent 5 years are made once a year, coincident with annual benchmark adjustments.

Caution on aggregating state data. State estimation procedures are designed to produce accurate data for each individual state. BLS independently develops a national employment series; state estimates are not forced to sum to national totals. Because each state series is subject to larger sampling and nonsampling errors than the national series, summing them cumulates individual state level errors and can cause significant distortions at an aggregate level. Due to these statistical limitations, BLS does not compile a "sum-of-states" employment series, and cautions users that such a series is subject to a relatively large and volatile error structure.

Reliability of the estimates

The estimates presented in this release are based on sample surveys, administrative data, and modeling and, thus, are subject to sampling and other types of errors. Sampling error is a measure of sampling variability—that is, variation that occurs by chance because a sample rather than the entire population is surveyed. Survey data also are subject to nonsampling errors, such as those which can be introduced into the data collection and processing operations. Estimates not directly derived from sample surveys are subject to additional errors resulting from the specific estimation processes used. The sums of individual items may not always equal the totals shown in the same tables because of rounding. Unemployment rates are computed from unrounded data and thus may differ slightly from rates computed using the rounded data displayed in the tables.

Use of error measures. The introductory section of this release preserves the long-time practice of highlighting the direction of the movements in regional and state unemployment rates and state nonfarm payroll employment regardless of their statistical significance. The remainder of the analysis in the release takes statistical significance into consideration.

Labor force and unemployment estimates. Model-based error measures for seasonally adjusted and not seasonally adjusted data and for over-the-month and over-the-year changes are available online at www.bls.gov/lau/lastderr.htm. BLS uses a 90-percent confidence level in determining whether changes in LAUS unemployment rates are statistically significant. The average magnitude of the current year over-the-month change in a state unemployment rate that is required for statistical significance at the 90-percent confidence level is just over 0.2 percentage point; the average amount of the current over-the-year change in a state rate for significance is about 0.3 point. More details can be found on the website. Measures of nonsampling error are not available.

Employment estimates. Measures of sampling error for state CES data at the total nonfarm and supersector levels are available online at www.bls.gov/sae/790stderr.htm. BLS uses a 90-percent confidence level in determining whether changes in CES employment levels are statistically significant. Information on recent benchmark revisions for states is available online at www.bls.gov/sae/.

Additional information

Estimates of labor force and unemployment from the LAUS program, as well as nonfarm employment from the CES program, for 394 metropolitan areas and metropolitan New England City and Town Areas (NECTAs) are available in the news release, Metropolitan Area Employment and Unemployment. Estimates of labor force, employment, and unemployment for approximately 7,500 subnational areas are available online at www.bls.gov/lau/. Employment data from the CES program for states and metropolitan areas are available online at www.bls.gov/sae/. Information in this release will be made available to sensory impaired individuals upon request. Voice phone: (202) 691-5200; Federal Relay Service: (800) 877-8339.

Table 1. Civilian labor force and unemployment by census region and division, seasonally adjusted [1]

(Numbers in thousands)

Census region and division	Civilian labor force				Unemployed							
					Number				Percent of labor force			
	Jan. 2014	Nov. 2014	Dec. 2014	Jan. 2015	Jan. 2014	Nov. 2014	Dec. 2014	Jan. 2015	Jan. 2014	Nov. 2014	Dec. 2014	Jan. 2015
Northeast	28,263.3	28,256.1	28,258.4	28,295.9	1,897.9	1,617.7	1,603.3	1,586.3	6.7	5.7	5.7	5.6
New England	7,751.0	7,816.4	7,821.1	7,829.2	493.5	433.6	429.5	418.0	6.4	5.5	5.5	5.3
Middle Atlantic	20,512.3	20,439.6	20,437.3	20,466.7	1,404.4	1,184.1	1,173.8	1,168.4	6.8	5.8	5.7	5.7
South	56,864.9	57,055.2	57,050.4	57,140.3	3,624.0	3,231.2	3,194.7	3,131.8	6.4	5.7	5.6	5.5
South Atlantic	30,151.8	30,252.8	30,242.8	30,290.6	1,974.7	1,775.4	1,752.3	1,721.1	6.5	5.9	5.8	5.7
East South Central	8,486.8	8,329.1	8,316.8	8,332.5	618.4	534.6	529.6	525.4	7.3	6.4	6.4	6.3
West South Central	18,226.3	18,473.4	18,490.8	18,517.2	1,030.9	921.2	912.8	885.2	5.7	5.0	4.9	4.8
Midwest	34,364.2	34,532.4	34,552.3	34,612.2	2,257.9	1,855.8	1,840.0	1,815.5	6.6	5.4	5.3	5.2
East North Central	23,291.0	23,368.6	23,379.7	23,417.4	1,708.4	1,376.2	1,363.1	1,341.7	7.3	5.9	5.8	5.7
West North Central	11,073.3	11,163.8	11,172.6	11,194.8	549.5	479.6	476.9	473.7	5.0	4.3	4.3	4.2
West	36,319.1	36,712.9	36,745.4	36,821.6	2,649.4	2,360.6	2,350.2	2,309.2	7.3	6.4	6.4	6.3
Mountain	11,188.9	11,302.6	11,311.8	11,342.6	711.2	609.1	604.0	595.5	6.4	5.4	5.3	5.3
Pacific	25,130.2	25,410.3	25,433.6	25,479.0	1,938.2	1,751.6	1,746.2	1,713.7	7.7	6.9	6.9	6.7

[1] Census region estimates are derived by summing the census division model-based estimates.

NOTE: Data refer to place of residence. The states (including the District of Columbia) that compose the various census divisions are: New England: Connecticut, Maine, Massachusetts, New Hampshire, Rhode Island, and Vermont; Middle Atlantic: New Jersey, New York, and Pennsylvania; South Atlantic: Delaware, District of Columbia, Florida, Georgia, Maryland, North Carolina, South Carolina, Virginia, and West Virginia; East South Central: Alabama, Kentucky, Mississippi, and Tennessee; West South Central: Arkansas, Louisiana, Oklahoma, and Texas; East North Central: Illinois, Indiana, Michigan, Ohio, and Wisconsin; West North Central: Iowa, Kansas, Minnesota, Missouri, Nebraska, North Dakota, and South Dakota; Mountain: Arizona, Colorado, Idaho, Montana, Nevada, New Mexico, Utah, and Wyoming; and Pacific: Alaska, California, Hawaii, Oregon, and Washington. Estimates for the current year are subject to revision early in the following calendar year.

Table 2. Civilian labor force and unemployment by census region and division, not seasonally adjusted [1]

(Numbers in thousands)

Census region and division	Civilian labor force				Unemployed							
					Number				Percent of labor force			
	December		January		December		January		December		January	
	2013	2014	2014	2015	2013	2014	2014	2015	2013	2014	2014	2015
Northeast	28,042.8	28,106.9	28,061.6	28,152.7	1,804.9	1,476.2	2,018.1	1,759.2	6.4	5.3	7.2	6.2
New England	7,709.3	7,789.9	7,696.6	7,771.1	472.0	394.7	537.1	455.7	6.1	5.1	7.0	5.9
Middle Atlantic	20,333.5	20,317.1	20,365.1	20,381.6	1,332.9	1,081.6	1,481.0	1,303.5	6.6	5.3	7.3	6.4
South	56,414.6	56,747.4	56,403.9	56,851.2	3,436.3	2,936.1	3,679.8	3,270.2	6.1	5.2	6.5	5.8
South Atlantic	29,842.9	30,043.0	29,903.9	30,149.1	1,881.0	1,628.8	1,992.4	1,791.9	6.3	5.4	6.7	5.9
East South Central	8,459.9	8,288.4	8,403.0	8,295.4	578.5	485.9	634.2	562.3	6.8	5.9	7.5	6.8
West South Central	18,111.9	18,416.1	18,097.0	18,406.7	976.8	821.4	1,053.2	916.0	5.4	4.5	5.8	5.0
Midwest	34,095.3	34,354.1	34,025.8	34,341.8	2,164.9	1,690.2	2,403.6	2,032.7	6.3	4.9	7.1	5.9
East North Central	23,117.1	23,236.5	23,038.8	23,227.2	1,646.5	1,240.6	1,789.9	1,490.4	7.1	5.3	7.8	6.4
West North Central	10,978.2	11,117.6	10,987.0	11,114.6	518.4	449.7	613.7	542.3	4.7	4.0	5.6	4.9
West	36,112.0	36,636.4	36,150.5	36,703.8	2,595.3	2,247.8	2,771.9	2,435.7	7.2	6.1	7.7	6.6
Mountain	11,137.4	11,285.4	11,135.4	11,305.6	697.2	576.2	747.1	634.3	6.3	5.1	6.7	5.6
Pacific	24,974.6	25,351.0	25,015.1	25,398.3	1,898.1	1,671.5	2,024.8	1,801.4	7.6	6.6	8.1	7.1

[1] Census region estimates are derived by summing the census division model-based estimates.

NOTE: Data refer to place of residence. The composition of the regions and divisions is described in table 1. Estimates for the current year are subject to revision early in the following calendar year.

Table 3. Civilian labor force and unemployment by state and selected area, seasonally adjusted

(Numbers in thousands)

| State and area | Civilian labor force | | | | Unemployed | | | | | | | |
| | | | | | Number | | | | Percent of labor force | | | |
	Jan. 2014	Nov. 2014	Dec. 2014	Jan. 2015p	Jan. 2014	Nov. 2014	Dec. 2014	Jan. 2015p	Jan. 2014	Nov. 2014	Dec. 2014	Jan. 2015p
Alabama	2,147.5	2,130.1	2,130.7	2,135.4	155.0	130.9	129.6	128.5	7.2	6.1	6.1	6.0
Alaska	366.7	366.0	365.7	366.6	25.2	23.9	23.5	23.0	6.9	6.5	6.4	6.3
Arizona	3,059.1	3,115.8	3,123.6	3,146.5	218.5	206.6	207.5	208.0	7.1	6.6	6.6	6.6
Arkansas	1,294.7	1,309.7	1,312.4	1,321.6	85.6	74.8	74.3	74.4	6.6	5.7	5.7	5.6
California	18,688.2	18,901.3	18,913.7	18,936.2	1,509.6	1,355.9	1,347.4	1,315.9	8.1	7.2	7.1	6.9
Los Angeles-Long Beach-Glendale [1]	4,995.7	5,049.2	5,051.3	5,058.5	437.9	403.9	402.8	397.4	8.8	8.0	8.0	7.9
Colorado	2,789.7	2,823.6	2,824.2	2,827.7	160.8	121.6	119.6	118.2	5.8	4.3	4.2	4.2
Connecticut	1,875.0	1,896.5	1,899.4	1,904.5	133.3	119.7	119.9	120.4	7.1	6.3	6.3	6.3
Delaware	445.2	455.2	455.3	456.2	26.9	24.1	23.6	22.8	6.1	5.3	5.2	5.0
District of Columbia	371.8	383.8	384.7	385.4	29.4	29.6	29.6	29.7	7.9	7.7	7.7	7.7
Florida	9,498.6	9,647.6	9,662.5	9,698.3	619.9	554.7	553.6	551.4	6.5	5.7	5.7	5.7
Miami-Miami Beach-Kendall [1]	1,304.0	1,328.9	1,329.6	1,330.7	94.3	84.1	83.3	80.8	7.2	6.3	6.3	6.1
Georgia	4,719.2	4,743.5	4,744.4	4,754.9	346.1	315.8	311.0	304.9	7.3	6.7	6.6	6.4
Hawaii	663.1	670.7	670.8	673.5	31.2	27.3	27.1	27.4	4.7	4.1	4.0	4.1
Idaho	773.7	777.1	776.5	778.5	39.4	34.9	34.1	31.9	5.1	4.5	4.4	4.1
Illinois	6,553.3	6,514.7	6,516.2	6,522.5	535.1	405.7	401.8	398.5	8.2	6.2	6.2	6.1
Chicago-Naperville-Arlington Heights [1]	3,795.6	3,802.3	3,806.7	3,810.0	322.2	236.9	233.8	233.8	8.5	6.2	6.1	6.1
Indiana	3,208.8	3,250.6	3,253.6	3,267.8	198.5	190.6	192.1	197.2	6.2	5.9	5.9	6.0
Iowa	1,690.8	1,714.7	1,715.6	1,716.5	74.4	73.7	73.6	71.5	4.4	4.3	4.3	4.2
Kansas	1,492.1	1,502.8	1,503.4	1,503.1	69.7	63.3	63.0	63.2	4.7	4.2	4.2	4.2
Kentucky	2,020.6	1,974.4	1,973.5	1,981.3	150.9	109.2	107.7	108.6	7.5	5.5	5.5	5.5
Louisiana	2,110.8	2,195.5	2,200.5	2,203.1	115.1	157.1	159.4	153.7	5.5	7.2	7.2	7.0
Maine	704.6	694.4	693.7	692.2	42.4	38.3	38.0	36.0	6.0	5.5	5.5	5.2
Maryland	3,102.1	3,104.6	3,104.8	3,112.0	187.2	172.2	171.1	172.2	6.0	5.5	5.5	5.5
Massachusetts	3,526.5	3,582.8	3,586.6	3,591.4	214.5	193.5	191.4	181.7	6.1	5.4	5.3	5.1
Michigan	4,748.0	4,748.0	4,747.8	4,762.7	375.1	309.1	305.6	298.4	7.9	6.5	6.4	6.3
Detroit-Warren-Dearborn [2]	2,023.2	2,019.0	2,018.9	2,018.8	190.4	157.4	155.0	149.0	9.4	7.8	7.7	7.4
Minnesota	2,972.5	2,976.0	2,976.6	2,988.0	133.9	109.3	109.8	110.1	4.5	3.7	3.7	3.7
Mississippi	1,240.7	1,220.6	1,220.3	1,227.3	98.0	88.0	87.7	87.6	7.9	7.2	7.2	7.1
Missouri	3,032.5	3,078.6	3,082.1	3,096.6	193.5	168.1	167.0	169.4	6.4	5.5	5.4	5.5
Montana	516.3	516.0	515.9	518.8	25.9	23.5	23.4	23.1	5.0	4.6	4.5	4.4
Nebraska	1,022.4	1,021.2	1,020.9	1,020.8	35.5	31.5	31.1	29.9	3.5	3.1	3.1	2.9
Nevada	1,387.2	1,397.9	1,398.8	1,401.7	117.6	99.5	98.5	99.3	8.5	7.1	7.0	7.1
New Hampshire	742.6	741.1	741.3	742.6	34.5	29.9	29.6	29.4	4.6	4.0	4.0	4.0
New Jersey	4,490.9	4,537.8	4,540.5	4,548.4	317.4	286.4	284.7	286.8	7.1	6.3	6.3	6.3
New Mexico	918.8	916.6	916.7	918.6	61.9	55.9	55.1	54.4	6.7	6.1	6.0	5.9
New York	9,612.1	9,533.8	9,532.0	9,553.2	657.7	557.4	554.9	554.9	6.8	5.8	5.8	5.8
New York City	4,114.7	4,128.9	4,131.8	4,148.5	329.6	269.7	268.7	271.2	8.0	6.5	6.5	6.5
North Carolina	4,638.1	4,625.5	4,625.3	4,646.8	306.0	255.4	250.0	248.9	6.6	5.5	5.4	5.4
North Dakota	410.1	421.2	421.8	422.3	11.3	11.7	11.7	11.9	2.7	2.8	2.8	2.8
Ohio	5,732.7	5,727.9	5,725.8	5,747.1	370.5	295.7	292.4	292.5	6.5	5.2	5.1	5.1
Cleveland-Elyria [2]	1,046.2	1,047.5	1,047.5	1,050.1	71.5	59.5	58.9	58.2	6.8	5.7	5.6	5.5
Oklahoma	1,792.6	1,781.5	1,782.2	1,794.7	89.1	71.1	69.9	69.4	5.0	4.0	3.9	3.9
Oregon	1,917.4	1,961.0	1,963.2	1,964.5	137.8	132.4	131.2	123.8	7.2	6.8	6.7	6.3
Pennsylvania	6,388.3	6,351.9	6,351.8	6,365.0	404.9	322.7	319.3	322.3	6.3	5.1	5.0	5.1
Rhode Island	555.1	549.7	548.8	548.8	47.5	37.9	37.2	35.7	8.6	6.9	6.8	6.5
South Carolina	2,169.5	2,212.9	2,216.3	2,227.0	136.0	146.6	147.1	147.0	6.3	6.6	6.6	6.6
South Dakota	447.1	448.8	448.8	449.2	15.7	14.9	15.0	15.1	3.5	3.3	3.3	3.4
Tennessee	3,010.1	2,983.0	2,982.6	3,012.0	200.4	196.9	196.4	201.7	6.7	6.6	6.6	6.7
Texas	13,018.7	13,161.1	13,171.8	13,186.0	717.3	609.7	601.8	585.1	5.5	4.6	4.6	4.4
Utah	1,420.9	1,440.2	1,442.2	1,446.7	55.8	51.8	51.3	49.8	3.9	3.6	3.6	3.4
Vermont	349.4	348.8	348.8	348.7	14.3	14.5	14.5	14.2	4.1	4.2	4.1	4.1
Virginia	4,242.2	4,234.2	4,233.9	4,244.1	226.0	204.5	202.8	199.6	5.3	4.8	4.8	4.7
Washington	3,463.2	3,517.4	3,522.8	3,535.7	223.5	221.9	223.3	224.8	6.5	6.3	6.3	6.4
Seattle-Bellevue-Everett [1]	1,544.8	1,562.3	1,564.1	1,566.7	77.1	71.5	71.4	72.5	5.0	4.6	4.6	4.6
West Virginia	794.8	778.2	776.5	774.4	53.7	46.6	45.7	45.6	6.8	6.0	5.9	5.9
Wisconsin	3,089.2	3,111.0	3,113.1	3,119.9	183.8	162.6	161.8	156.4	6.0	5.2	5.2	5.0
Wyoming	306.7	306.4	306.2	305.9	13.2	13.1	12.9	12.3	4.3	4.3	4.2	4.0
Puerto Rico	1,169.6	1,138.6	1,138.7	1,136.3	174.2	157.0	156.1	140.9	14.9	13.8	13.7	12.4

[1] Metropolitan division.
[2] Metropolitan statistical area.
p = preliminary.
NOTE: Data refer to place of residence. Data for Puerto Rico are derived from a monthly household survey similar to the Current Population Survey. Area definitions are based on Office of Management and Budget Bulletin No. 13-01, dated February 28, 2013, and are available on the BLS website at www.bls.gov/lau/lausmsa.htm. Estimates for the latest month are subject to revision the following month.

Table 4. Civilian labor force and unemployment by state and selected area, not seasonally adjusted

(Numbers in thousands)

State and area	Civilian labor force				Unemployed							
					Number				Percent of labor force			
	December		January		December		January		December		January	
	2013	2014	2014	2015p	2013	2014	2014	2015p	2013	2014	2014	2015p
Alabama	2,153.6	2,122.7	2,148.6	2,104.5	142.9	117.5	162.6	132.4	6.6	5.5	7.6	6.3
Alaska	362.1	362.5	362.5	362.3	25.2	23.3	27.9	25.8	7.0	6.4	7.7	7.1
Arizona	3,053.8	3,124.4	3,052.2	3,142.9	216.7	197.1	222.4	207.5	7.1	6.3	7.3	6.6
Arkansas	1,286.1	1,304.1	1,273.1	1,309.9	88.1	72.2	94.6	85.0	6.8	5.5	7.4	6.5
California	18,602.2	18,855.7	18,646.8	18,889.1	1,481.3	1,277.5	1,575.9	1,371.3	8.0	6.8	8.5	7.3
Los Angeles-Long Beach-Glendale [1]	4,988.9	5,047.0	4,980.2	5,048.8	426.4	379.6	445.8	409.9	8.5	7.5	9.0	8.1
Colorado	2,773.2	2,815.1	2,780.6	2,809.4	164.6	115.9	178.7	131.4	5.9	4.1	6.4	4.7
Connecticut	1,856.9	1,887.2	1,858.1	1,888.0	124.3	105.9	140.4	127.8	6.7	5.6	7.6	6.8
Delaware	444.8	455.8	444.0	455.0	25.3	21.1	29.1	24.8	5.7	4.6	6.6	5.4
District of Columbia	371.2	382.0	370.7	384.6	28.2	28.4	29.9	30.9	7.6	7.4	8.1	8.0
Florida	9,437.8	9,607.7	9,479.9	9,629.9	597.5	516.9	629.4	554.5	6.3	5.4	6.6	5.8
Miami-Miami Beach-Kendall [1]	1,292.9	1,322.9	1,312.2	1,339.4	87.1	77.6	90.6	77.7	6.7	5.9	6.9	5.8
Georgia	4,732.7	4,748.4	4,722.0	4,746.4	347.2	298.4	352.1	310.4	7.3	6.3	7.5	6.5
Hawaii	660.8	670.6	664.0	676.1	28.9	25.0	31.4	28.8	4.4	3.7	4.7	4.3
Idaho	768.6	771.8	768.3	773.3	41.2	33.6	47.4	37.2	5.4	4.4	6.2	4.8
Illinois	6,496.5	6,491.4	6,489.7	6,456.3	534.1	373.8	572.9	443.9	8.2	5.8	8.8	6.9
Chicago-Naperville-Arlington Heights [1]	3,758.3	3,777.3	3,763.0	3,778.7	308.2	210.3	329.7	258.7	8.2	5.6	8.8	6.8
Indiana	3,184.1	3,239.6	3,166.5	3,253.9	202.2	186.2	207.6	218.5	6.3	5.7	6.6	6.7
Iowa	1,679.0	1,706.5	1,682.3	1,702.0	75.6	74.7	90.7	82.8	4.5	4.4	5.4	4.9
Kansas	1,482.9	1,500.5	1,486.6	1,489.0	64.5	56.6	77.1	69.0	4.4	3.8	5.2	4.6
Kentucky	2,026.3	1,966.8	2,012.9	1,959.4	142.3	99.3	161.0	119.1	7.0	5.1	8.0	6.1
Louisiana	2,089.2	2,180.3	2,080.0	2,173.0	107.4	141.0	121.7	151.5	5.1	6.5	5.9	7.0
Maine	701.1	689.7	695.3	681.9	42.6	36.7	48.9	39.9	6.1	5.3	7.0	5.9
Maryland	3,092.7	3,091.6	3,088.1	3,100.4	179.9	160.6	196.2	183.3	5.8	5.2	6.4	5.9
Massachusetts	3,506.8	3,576.9	3,503.6	3,565.7	211.4	176.0	240.3	198.2	6.0	4.9	6.9	5.6
Michigan	4,687.9	4,711.6	4,679.5	4,722.0	362.3	263.6	393.8	313.1	7.7	5.6	8.4	6.6
Detroit-Warren-Dearborn [2]	2,004.9	2,003.3	1,998.3	1,998.7	170.9	129.4	185.6	147.1	8.5	6.5	9.3	7.4
Minnesota	2,955.3	2,964.8	2,950.8	2,979.4	131.8	105.3	160.4	136.4	4.5	3.6	5.4	4.6
Mississippi	1,254.0	1,225.5	1,240.9	1,222.5	97.6	87.3	107.2	95.8	7.8	7.1	8.6	7.8
Missouri	2,997.8	3,068.4	3,011.3	3,073.5	184.9	156.8	212.4	188.5	6.2	5.1	7.1	6.1
Montana	511.8	510.2	510.5	518.3	27.6	23.3	31.2	27.6	5.4	4.6	6.1	5.3
Nebraska	1,016.8	1,015.7	1,012.8	1,011.8	34.3	29.4	41.0	33.2	3.4	2.9	4.0	3.3
Nevada	1,380.2	1,395.2	1,384.7	1,395.9	117.4	96.0	123.2	105.2	8.5	6.9	8.9	7.5
New Hampshire	740.2	739.2	739.0	740.7	33.8	28.3	38.3	33.7	4.6	3.8	5.2	4.5
New Jersey	4,465.9	4,522.8	4,459.5	4,520.4	301.0	264.3	336.8	314.5	6.7	5.8	7.6	7.0
New Mexico	924.8	922.6	915.6	918.8	60.4	52.0	65.0	57.3	6.5	5.6	7.1	6.2
New York	9,519.4	9,471.7	9,552.7	9,519.1	638.2	525.9	706.4	618.0	6.7	5.6	7.4	6.5
New York City	4,082.8	4,121.5	4,102.4	4,148.4	316.6	255.9	339.7	293.3	7.8	6.2	8.3	7.1
North Carolina	4,614.8	4,594.0	4,622.6	4,636.7	301.3	231.7	317.6	273.2	6.5	5.0	6.9	5.9
North Dakota	403.5	416.3	403.7	416.3	11.3	11.7	14.0	15.0	2.8	2.8	3.5	3.6
Ohio	5,682.3	5,697.3	5,652.1	5,704.3	364.5	270.5	418.3	346.5	6.4	4.7	7.4	6.1
Cleveland-Elyria [2]	1,032.6	1,033.7	1,037.6	1,045.6	65.5	53.3	75.8	63.1	6.3	5.2	7.3	6.0
Oklahoma	1,788.1	1,779.4	1,778.6	1,796.8	90.0	68.0	95.3	76.7	5.0	3.8	5.4	4.3
Oregon	1,901.8	1,951.3	1,899.9	1,942.7	135.1	124.5	149.3	128.1	7.1	6.4	7.9	6.6
Pennsylvania	6,348.2	6,322.6	6,352.8	6,342.1	393.7	291.4	437.8	371.0	6.2	4.6	6.9	5.8
Rhode Island	555.6	548.8	552.8	548.5	46.4	34.4	52.8	40.2	8.3	6.3	9.6	7.3
South Carolina	2,150.1	2,191.9	2,149.9	2,210.6	134.8	139.4	139.9	152.0	6.3	6.4	6.5	6.9
South Dakota	442.9	445.3	439.6	442.6	16.0	15.3	18.2	17.3	3.6	3.4	4.1	3.9
Tennessee	3,026.0	2,973.3	3,000.6	3,009.0	195.7	181.7	203.4	214.9	6.5	6.1	6.8	7.1
Texas	12,948.4	13,152.2	12,965.4	13,126.9	691.4	540.1	741.6	602.8	5.3	4.1	5.7	4.6
Utah	1,419.3	1,441.3	1,418.7	1,442.9	55.0	45.6	63.1	53.8	3.9	3.2	4.5	3.7
Vermont	348.8	348.1	347.8	346.3	13.7	13.4	16.4	15.9	3.9	3.8	4.7	4.6
Virginia	4,211.5	4,204.1	4,236.8	4,223.7	216.2	189.6	238.4	209.7	5.1	4.5	5.6	5.0
Washington	3,447.8	3,510.9	3,441.8	3,528.0	227.6	221.3	240.3	247.4	6.6	6.3	7.0	7.0
Seattle-Bellevue-Everett [1]	1,535.8	1,556.4	1,530.6	1,555.7	72.3	66.6	76.6	76.8	4.7	4.3	5.0	4.9
West Virginia	787.2	767.4	790.0	761.8	50.7	42.8	59.9	53.1	6.4	5.6	7.6	7.0
Wisconsin	3,066.2	3,096.5	3,051.1	3,090.8	183.5	146.4	197.3	168.4	6.0	4.7	6.5	5.4
Wyoming	305.7	304.7	304.9	304.0	14.3	12.8	16.1	14.4	4.7	4.2	5.3	4.8
Puerto Rico	1,186.1	1,140.4	1,178.3	1,146.2	182.1	137.7	169.6	124.4	15.4	12.1	14.4	10.8

[1] Metropolitan division.
[2] Metropolitan statistical area.
p = preliminary.
NOTE: Data refer to place of residence. Data for Puerto Rico are derived from a monthly household survey similar to the Current Population Survey. Area definitions are based on Office of Management and Budget Bulletin No. 13-01, dated February 28, 2013, and are available at www.bls.gov/lau/lausmsa.htm. Estimates for the latest month are subject to revision the following month.

Table 5. Employees on nonfarm payrolls by state and selected industry sector, seasonally adjusted

[In thousands]

State	Total[1]				Construction				Manufacturing			
	Jan. 2014	Nov. 2014	Dec. 2014	Jan. 2015[p]	Jan. 2014	Nov. 2014	Dec. 2014	Jan. 2015[p]	Jan. 2014	Nov. 2014	Dec. 2014	Jan. 2015[p]
Alabama[2]	1,910.3	1,940.6	1,942.8	1,945.2	79.3	80.3	81.0	80.6	–	–	–	–
Alaska	337.7	338.1	340.6	341.6	17.4	17.8	18.1	18.4	15.1	13.5	14.5	14.0
Arizona	2,546.2	2,598.6	2,607.3	2,614.2	126.7	126.5	126.7	129.5	156.1	156.2	156.1	156.6
Arkansas	1,179.8	1,199.1	1,204.6	1,206.6	46.5	46.5	47.4	49.7	152.9	157.2	157.4	155.6
California	15,430.0	15,840.9	15,860.7	15,928.0	660.4	694.5	686.5	698.2	1,264.8	1,272.3	1,271.7	1,267.5
Colorado	2,425.4	2,484.2	2,492.8	2,496.5	137.4	145.1	148.2	150.9	134.3	138.7	138.4	138.5
Connecticut	1,659.9	1,672.9	1,678.1	1,684.5	53.9	55.7	54.9	56.2	160.9	158.5	159.7	158.8
Delaware[3]	435.6	442.3	442.8	442.5	19.9	20.3	20.1	19.8	25.6	25.8	25.7	25.8
District of Columbia[2, 3]	748.1	762.3	761.4	760.2	14.2	14.5	14.5	14.5	–	–	–	–
Florida	7,705.5	7,945.2	7,965.7	7,979.6	383.6	408.4	409.9	415.4	327.6	332.8	331.8	330.1
Georgia	4,090.2	4,216.2	4,226.5	4,222.1	152.8	158.9	158.2	155.4	361.2	371.4	370.4	374.3
Hawaii[3]	627.4	625.6	626.0	631.5	31.2	31.3	30.9	32.0	13.6	13.5	13.4	13.7
Idaho	648.2	659.1	659.1	668.4	34.7	36.7	37.4	39.1	60.1	59.2	59.5	60.6
Illinois	5,834.9	5,891.5	5,907.0	5,899.9	196.3	205.6	209.9	207.4	578.7	579.3	581.0	578.9
Indiana	2,951.9	3,005.1	3,012.1	3,017.6	122.0	122.8	122.9	120.1	501.0	514.1	514.6	516.1
Iowa	1,537.4	1,557.4	1,559.1	1,562.2	70.1	77.1	77.5	76.6	216.7	215.5	216.7	216.8
Kansas	1,382.0	1,398.9	1,401.9	1,399.3	60.4	59.8	60.7	60.9	160.5	162.0	162.5	159.0
Kentucky	1,843.7	1,879.3	1,880.0	1,883.9	70.3	73.8	74.3	74.9	231.3	236.8	237.5	240.3
Louisiana	1,964.4	1,994.4	1,996.6	1,989.1	133.7	142.5	141.7	137.6	146.3	148.4	148.7	150.0
Maine	601.9	604.8	604.7	601.3	25.8	25.9	26.0	25.3	49.9	50.7	50.7	49.8
Maryland[3]	2,603.0	2,636.3	2,641.3	2,641.8	149.2	152.7	153.5	153.2	103.9	102.6	103.0	102.5
Massachusetts	3,380.5	3,436.8	3,445.9	3,448.5	124.8	128.4	128.3	129.5	251.2	249.2	248.6	248.8
Michigan	4,143.5	4,207.3	4,217.6	4,241.8	137.3	142.7	144.6	150.5	566.2	584.8	584.9	589.8
Minnesota	2,795.2	2,830.6	2,831.4	2,823.5	104.8	106.0	105.8	104.1	309.4	315.5	315.8	314.7
Mississippi	1,120.1	1,122.6	1,124.5	1,129.1	51.8	45.9	45.9	45.2	139.3	139.5	139.4	139.4
Missouri	2,715.7	2,740.2	2,744.6	2,758.9	109.8	109.2	110.7	110.6	249.3	260.6	260.8	261.7
Montana	453.2	453.8	454.7	456.7	24.6	24.3	25.6	25.3	18.9	19.2	19.0	18.8
Nebraska[3]	989.3	996.0	996.8	1,001.5	46.2	47.0	46.8	46.0	97.2	97.3	96.5	97.3
Nevada	1,193.8	1,228.4	1,230.5	1,237.2	60.1	63.2	64.2	65.5	41.6	41.9	42.2	42.0
New Hampshire	645.9	651.5	653.0	650.2	23.1	23.7	24.0	24.3	66.5	67.0	67.1	66.9
New Jersey	3,945.6	3,982.1	3,982.3	3,994.7	138.1	144.3	144.3	150.4	243.3	241.6	242.0	243.2
New Mexico	816.0	828.8	827.4	828.9	42.9	43.2	43.1	43.7	28.6	28.2	28.4	28.4
New York	9,008.6	9,134.8	9,156.3	9,166.3	331.3	340.9	346.9	347.7	455.0	451.5	450.9	449.2
North Carolina	4,095.4	4,187.8	4,203.1	4,203.1	175.9	182.2	184.4	187.2	444.7	455.0	455.2	458.6
North Dakota	451.0	469.1	469.2	470.5	32.1	36.0	36.8	36.4	25.8	26.1	26.4	26.2
Ohio	5,297.2	5,364.8	5,369.9	5,395.0	189.4	192.9	193.5	192.1	668.3	677.4	677.2	680.8
Oklahoma[2]	1,644.7	1,665.6	1,668.3	1,669.4	76.0	77.0	77.5	77.6	–	–	–	–
Oregon	1,697.4	1,741.5	1,745.4	1,753.0	78.4	79.3	79.8	81.2	177.2	181.3	182.0	184.2
Pennsylvania	5,759.6	5,816.2	5,825.5	5,822.0	227.5	235.8	232.1	233.2	566.2	568.6	570.8	571.4
Rhode Island	475.1	478.7	479.3	481.6	16.3	16.4	16.6	16.9	40.6	41.2	41.4	41.1
South Carolina	1,928.2	1,972.8	1,975.2	1,979.4	81.5	83.0	83.7	83.2	227.2	232.4	233.3	231.6
South Dakota[3]	422.0	423.9	424.7	424.8	22.2	22.0	22.5	22.7	41.6	42.9	43.2	43.5
Tennessee[3]	2,787.5	2,841.1	2,850.9	2,859.2	109.2	113.4	115.5	114.9	322.3	328.8	330.6	332.3
Texas	11,376.7	11,703.3	11,749.5	11,769.6	628.7	669.9	677.9	678.3	875.7	891.4	891.2	892.1
Utah	1,310.7	1,344.8	1,353.6	1,363.3	76.2	79.3	81.2	83.6	119.8	120.7	121.3	122.7
Vermont	308.9	312.5	311.7	312.8	14.7	14.6	14.6	15.3	31.5	31.0	31.0	30.5
Virginia	3,759.6	3,795.7	3,797.3	3,786.4	175.6	179.9	178.4	179.5	231.8	232.0	232.9	233.6
Washington	3,040.8	3,113.7	3,122.6	3,140.9	155.2	166.2	167.7	172.5	288.0	290.5	291.0	291.1
West Virginia	761.3	761.5	763.1	764.5	33.3	31.7	32.3	32.6	48.0	47.7	47.5	48.1
Wisconsin	2,829.3	2,869.0	2,872.0	2,872.6	100.7	106.7	107.7	110.0	460.4	468.9	469.1	472.0
Wyoming	291.2	293.0	295.0	295.9	23.0	22.6	23.8	23.2	9.8	9.9	9.9	10.0
Puerto Rico[3]	916.7	907.9	908.2	905.8	27.8	27.1	28.5	26.3	75.5	74.9	74.9	73.4
Virgin Islands[2]	37.5	38.0	38.1	38.0	–	–	–	–	–	–	–	–

[1] Includes mining and logging, information, and other services (except public administration), not shown separately.

[2] Missing series (denoted by '-') are not published seasonally adjusted because the seasonal component, which is small relative to the trend-cycle and irregular components, cannot be separated with sufficient precision.

[3] Mining and logging is combined with construction.

p Preliminary

NOTE: Data are counts of jobs by place of work. Data have been revised to reflect 2014 benchmarks and updated seasonal adjustment factors. Seasonally adjusted data from January 2010 are subject to revision. Some seasonally adjusted series may have been revised back to 1990. Estimates subsequent to the current benchmark are preliminary and will be revised when new information becomes available.

Table 5. Employees on nonfarm payrolls by state and selected industry sector, seasonally adjusted-Continued

[In thousands]

State	Trade, transportation, and utilities				Financial activities				Professional and business services			
	Jan. 2014	Nov. 2014	Dec. 2014	Jan. 2015p	Jan. 2014	Nov. 2014	Dec. 2014	Jan. 2015p	Jan. 2014	Nov. 2014	Dec. 2014	Jan. 2015p
Alabama	371.1	376.8	378.6	374.9	94.7	94.8	94.7	96.3	220.2	225.6	225.3	229.8
Alaska	64.2	65.8	66.3	66.9	12.2	12.3	12.5	12.2	30.1	29.2	29.4	29.6
Arizona	488.4	498.2	501.6	498.7	187.9	190.6	190.5	191.2	375.4	389.5	391.8	395.8
Arkansas	242.3	248.4	248.9	249.2	49.6	49.7	49.5	49.6	131.1	134.7	134.9	135.8
California	2,831.5	2,907.6	2,914.3	2,917.1	780.5	790.9	793.0	797.8	2,385.3	2,485.0	2,493.4	2,497.2
Colorado	427.4	435.6	436.1	436.7	152.2	154.1	154.7	155.1	379.7	388.1	390.7	388.3
Connecticut	300.0	303.7	304.1	301.1	129.2	128.4	128.3	129.8	209.8	213.8	214.7	216.8
Delaware	79.0	80.0	80.4	80.4	44.5	46.1	46.3	46.5	59.1	61.2	61.4	61.9
District of Columbia	29.6	32.1	32.3	32.1	29.9	30.5	30.4	30.7	155.8	160.6	160.1	160.7
Florida	1,599.3	1,647.2	1,654.9	1,651.6	516.5	532.4	533.5	530.2	1,141.6	1,187.3	1,193.2	1,200.3
Georgia	858.8	886.6	891.7	892.3	230.1	234.0	234.6	237.1	601.8	631.1	631.8	626.7
Hawaii	117.0	117.7	118.0	119.9	27.3	27.5	27.6	27.5	81.8	83.6	83.7	85.0
Idaho	130.6	133.3	132.8	133.0	32.2	33.3	33.4	34.1	79.8	79.3	78.9	82.1
Illinois	1,168.0	1,175.2	1,176.9	1,178.5	369.6	369.1	368.5	368.2	902.0	921.3	924.2	918.7
Indiana	571.4	580.1	581.5	588.2	127.6	131.0	130.9	130.8	318.4	325.6	328.2	328.7
Iowa	311.8	315.7	315.2	317.4	104.0	104.7	104.6	104.4	134.7	136.4	137.1	138.9
Kansas	262.0	264.2	264.8	268.1	79.2	79.6	79.3	80.9	166.6	171.8	172.2	170.6
Kentucky	373.4	381.0	381.3	383.8	89.1	90.8	90.3	89.5	207.4	216.1	216.7	214.8
Louisiana	385.9	393.3	394.1	394.4	91.5	92.5	92.8	93.9	212.3	213.2	213.7	208.8
Maine	118.7	118.9	119.2	117.8	30.4	30.5	30.4	30.5	62.1	63.2	63.5	63.5
Maryland	453.1	456.7	457.4	458.4	144.3	144.2	144.2	144.3	418.3	427.4	427.0	428.9
Massachusetts	558.8	565.0	566.1	569.9	207.1	209.0	208.9	210.6	510.5	520.6	523.3	523.3
Michigan	751.8	761.6	761.1	765.2	204.0	204.7	206.1	206.8	607.2	629.1	633.4	639.4
Minnesota	513.4	518.2	520.9	514.9	178.2	179.8	179.0	179.1	351.2	357.3	357.7	359.9
Mississippi	219.1	221.0	221.8	225.2	43.3	44.4	44.3	44.4	100.9	101.8	102.9	104.5
Missouri	520.3	523.4	524.1	525.1	163.7	164.8	164.5	165.1	348.9	356.5	356.9	357.4
Montana	92.4	93.4	93.8	95.4	24.4	25.2	25.7	25.8	39.3	39.8	39.8	40.2
Nebraska	203.2	203.6	203.0	203.2	72.1	72.8	73.1	73.3	112.6	112.3	112.6	113.8
Nevada	226.1	231.8	232.5	235.1	57.1	57.1	57.1	56.3	152.3	159.9	159.0	161.1
New Hampshire	136.7	138.1	138.9	137.0	35.6	36.3	36.0	36.1	72.5	73.9	73.5	73.4
New Jersey	831.8	842.8	844.5	850.0	247.9	249.2	246.6	246.4	634.8	637.7	637.4	630.6
New Mexico	137.4	140.0	139.1	139.6	33.2	33.6	33.5	33.7	99.1	99.9	100.3	100.4
New York	1,545.3	1,563.6	1,566.9	1,568.7	687.6	689.8	691.0	694.0	1,212.8	1,238.3	1,242.5	1,241.4
North Carolina	769.0	786.0	790.2	778.5	208.5	212.8	213.9	214.7	555.4	584.7	587.8	588.4
North Dakota	104.1	107.7	107.1	108.2	23.7	24.2	24.2	24.5	34.9	37.0	36.3	36.3
Ohio	988.7	998.6	997.8	1,010.1	285.8	290.2	289.9	291.2	702.3	716.4	716.6	719.3
Oklahoma	299.7	303.0	303.9	302.5	79.3	79.8	79.7	80.0	183.0	190.4	191.1	193.9
Oregon	321.6	329.0	330.3	333.3	91.5	93.4	92.8	92.8	213.9	224.1	223.8	227.0
Pennsylvania	1,101.4	1,116.7	1,123.0	1,119.9	314.8	313.3	313.7	316.2	751.2	762.2	762.4	763.3
Rhode Island	74.6	75.6	75.4	75.9	32.4	32.4	32.5	32.6	59.5	60.7	60.6	61.3
South Carolina	368.4	377.8	379.6	382.4	96.2	96.9	96.7	97.3	249.1	260.7	261.3	260.8
South Dakota	84.9	85.4	85.9	86.3	29.9	29.6	29.5	29.5	30.3	29.9	29.9	30.4
Tennessee	585.1	596.8	598.6	602.0	139.9	142.3	142.2	142.9	365.3	378.5	381.2	381.6
Texas	2,279.9	2,339.1	2,348.1	2,359.0	692.0	710.3	713.2	713.8	1,508.5	1,564.9	1,576.1	1,580.9
Utah	250.0	257.2	261.0	261.3	73.8	76.4	76.9	77.3	182.8	189.3	189.9	194.0
Vermont	55.5	56.1	56.2	56.3	12.1	12.2	12.3	12.4	26.4	26.8	26.8	26.7
Virginia	641.4	654.0	654.6	643.9	192.7	193.5	193.6	193.6	673.9	677.4	676.5	673.6
Washington	562.0	578.8	579.5	582.2	152.3	155.8	156.5	158.1	365.4	377.9	379.7	383.3
West Virginia	135.1	135.2	135.9	136.3	31.2	31.1	30.9	30.8	64.8	67.8	68.3	68.7
Wisconsin	521.4	526.6	528.3	525.6	149.2	153.1	153.9	153.5	306.2	307.7	307.5	305.7
Wyoming	54.7	55.1	55.5	56.3	11.1	11.3	11.3	11.5	18.1	18.6	19.1	19.4
Puerto Rico	176.6	176.6	175.2	177.3	43.5	42.5	42.3	42.5	114.9	111.8	112.1	111.6
Virgin Islands[1]	8.2	8.2	8.1	8.1	-	-	-	-	-	-	-	-

[1] Missing series (denoted by '-') are not published seasonally adjusted because the seasonal component, which is small relative to the trend-cycle and irregular components, cannot be separated with sufficient precision.

p Preliminary

NOTE: Data are counts of jobs by place of work. Data have been revised to reflect 2014 benchmarks and updated seasonal adjustment factors. Seasonally adjusted data from January 2010 are subject to revision. Some seasonally adjusted series may have been revised back to 1990. Estimates subsequent to the current benchmark are preliminary and will be revised when new information becomes available.

ESTABLISHMENT DATA
SEASONALLY ADJUSTED
Table 5. Employees on nonfarm payrolls by state and selected industry sector, seasonally adjusted-Continued
[In thousands]

State	Education and health services				Leisure and hospitality				Government			
	Jan. 2014	Nov. 2014	Dec. 2014	Jan. 2015ᵖ	Jan. 2014	Nov. 2014	Dec. 2014	Jan. 2015ᵖ	Jan. 2014	Nov. 2014	Dec. 2014	Jan. 2015ᵖ
Alabama...........................	222.0	226.7	227.1	226.9	181.9	187.4	188.2	189.8	376.8	379.8	379.5	379.1
Alaska.............................	46.9	47.0	47.2	47.0	34.0	34.6	34.8	34.7	82.2	82.0	82.0	82.3
Arizona............................	376.0	387.4	389.9	391.4	281.8	292.5	292.6	294.4	411.1	410.9	411.1	407.0
Arkansas..........................	171.7	173.5	173.5	173.5	106.2	109.3	113.1	112.8	213.2	213.1	213.2	213.1
California..........................	2,375.5	2,440.2	2,443.9	2,457.7	1,726.8	1,777.4	1,784.5	1,794.7	2,392.4	2,432.7	2,431.7	2,442.9
Colorado...........................	292.3	303.0	304.4	307.4	295.1	304.8	306.1	308.9	405.8	409.3	409.1	406.4
Connecticut.......................	322.3	327.6	328.7	331.5	151.5	153.1	155.0	157.1	237.0	237.4	237.7	238.6
Delaware..........................	71.6	73.5	73.2	72.8	46.6	47.3	47.6	48.0	65.7	65.2	65.3	64.4
District of Columbia.............	127.5	129.9	129.7	126.5	68.6	70.0	70.0	69.4	234.7	236.1	236.3	236.9
Florida.............................	1,141.3	1,177.1	1,181.3	1,184.4	1,062.7	1,109.2	1,109.3	1,116.2	1,073.2	1,078.4	1,079.3	1,078.6
Georgia............................	515.6	529.9	533.0	533.2	421.1	441.7	444.6	443.4	681.3	688.5	687.5	687.4
Hawaii.............................	78.7	79.4	79.5	79.6	112.9	113.6	113.5	114.7	129.7	124.4	124.8	124.4
Idaho..............................	92.8	94.1	93.9	95.7	65.0	66.9	67.0	67.3	117.8	120.4	120.2	120.1
Illinois.............................	881.2	892.0	894.1	896.4	553.4	556.3	559.7	563.0	826.5	831.4	831.2	828.5
Indiana............................	436.1	441.2	441.5	442.4	290.9	294.2	295.0	295.2	417.4	427.4	429.2	426.1
Iowa...............................	221.1	224.1	223.7	222.4	137.8	139.3	139.7	140.5	254.2	258.1	257.7	259.1
Kansas............................	188.0	190.9	191.5	189.8	121.7	124.6	124.8	125.9	256.4	258.0	257.7	256.6
Kentucky..........................	260.9	265.1	264.2	264.3	181.4	184.8	185.4	187.5	322.9	324.6	324.6	323.5
Louisiana..........................	296.8	300.9	301.5	304.7	217.2	223.4	225.0	223.4	331.5	327.1	327.1	325.9
Maine..............................	122.0	122.8	123.0	122.0	62.8	61.9	61.4	62.2	99.4	100.0	99.7	99.3
Maryland..........................	422.9	432.6	434.5	434.0	257.7	263.5	265.5	262.7	502.7	506.9	506.7	507.5
Massachusetts....................	724.7	741.7	744.2	741.5	338.5	344.6	346.6	342.7	447.0	455.9	456.6	458.4
Michigan...........................	642.6	647.6	649.1	651.4	403.0	405.8	406.9	411.4	595.5	594.6	595.2	591.2
Minnesota.........................	495.2	502.6	501.6	503.1	252.6	256.4	256.7	256.9	417.8	420.7	418.6	417.7
Mississippi........................	133.9	136.7	136.6	136.6	125.6	126.5	126.7	126.5	244.6	245.5	245.5	245.4
Missouri...........................	432.9	434.3	434.4	436.0	284.6	285.2	287.3	292.4	432.3	432.1	431.5	433.8
Montana...........................	69.8	69.8	69.8	69.2	60.8	60.8	60.1	60.1	89.5	87.9	87.6	88.5
Nebraska..........................	147.1	149.9	150.3	151.0	87.7	87.1	88.7	89.7	169.3	171.6	171.7	171.6
Nevada............................	113.8	117.6	118.6	119.1	329.1	341.4	342.2	344.1	152.0	152.7	152.5	152.0
New Hampshire...................	115.0	116.3	117.1	116.9	66.9	67.2	67.3	66.8	90.8	90.5	90.3	89.6
New Jersey........................	630.5	638.7	640.5	644.0	357.3	358.6	358.2	361.1	618.0	622.6	622.5	623.1
New Mexico........................	125.5	130.5	131.3	131.5	90.2	91.2	90.5	90.4	192.2	191.8	191.6	191.6
New York..........................	1,827.3	1,868.9	1,871.6	1,885.5	859.5	874.9	879.7	870.9	1,428.1	1,440.4	1,439.3	1,433.2
North Carolina....................	561.5	572.1	572.4	572.1	440.1	449.1	451.4	456.6	715.5	714.2	715.8	713.8
North Dakota......................	59.1	60.2	59.7	59.4	39.9	41.6	41.7	41.9	80.0	80.5	80.6	80.9
Ohio...............................	884.7	890.1	890.2	900.3	522.9	541.1	547.1	550.2	759.0	759.4	760.2	752.0
Oklahoma..........................	227.5	229.0	230.0	230.5	154.7	155.3	155.0	153.8	347.5	348.1	348.0	348.0
Oregon............................	245.1	253.1	253.8	252.5	181.0	184.0	184.5	184.5	291.1	297.0	297.6	297.6
Pennsylvania......................	1,170.7	1,188.7	1,190.6	1,183.3	536.1	544.0	546.2	546.8	716.5	709.1	708.4	708.6
Rhode Island......................	105.0	105.1	104.9	104.8	54.6	55.4	55.6	56.3	60.2	60.0	60.1	60.1
South Carolina....................	223.1	227.5	227.8	228.4	227.6	232.5	230.3	233.4	353.8	359.2	360.0	359.4
South Dakota......................	68.2	68.7	68.6	68.7	45.5	45.3	45.0	44.3	77.5	78.2	78.0	77.6
Tennessee.........................	399.8	406.2	406.3	407.9	290.6	299.3	300.2	300.5	425.6	426.1	426.9	427.9
Texas..............................	1,505.8	1,546.9	1,553.1	1,553.5	1,164.7	1,212.1	1,212.5	1,214.3	1,819.1	1,836.3	1,841.3	1,842.6
Utah...............................	172.6	176.9	177.0	178.1	125.9	130.9	132.1	131.8	227.4	230.2	230.1	230.0
Vermont...........................	62.5	62.7	62.9	63.0	34.8	37.7	36.2	36.5	55.7	55.8	56.0	56.4
Virginia............................	493.3	498.6	499.3	503.0	369.8	376.1	377.3	375.4	704.7	707.4	708.2	707.0
Washington........................	448.9	458.9	460.2	460.8	296.6	297.4	297.5	302.5	545.6	554.5	557.0	556.8
West Virginia......................	126.9	127.0	126.5	127.6	74.2	72.3	72.7	72.4	152.2	153.8	153.8	152.6
Wisconsin.........................	427.6	433.1	433.1	432.7	263.9	265.9	267.9	267.0	410.1	414.7	412.3	412.6
Wyoming...........................	27.0	27.3	27.2	27.5	35.1	35.9	36.0	36.6	71.6	71.5	71.3	71.5
Puerto Rico........................	123.1	125.4	125.3	126.7	79.8	80.1	80.4	80.2	237.0	231.6	231.6	230.5
Virgin Islands[1]..................	–	–	–	–	7.2	7.3	7.3	7.3	10.8	10.9	10.9	10.9

[1] Missing series (denoted by '-') are not published seasonally adjusted because the seasonal component, which is small relative to the trend-cycle and irregular components, cannot be separated with sufficient precision.

p Preliminary

NOTE: Data are counts of jobs by place of work. Data have been revised to reflect 2014 benchmarks and updated seasonal adjustment factors. Seasonally adjusted data from January 2010 are subject to revision. Some seasonally adjusted series may have been revised back to 1990. Estimates subsequent to the current benchmark are preliminary and will be revised when new information becomes available.

Table 6. Employees on nonfarm payrolls by state and selected industry sector, not seasonally adjusted
[In thousands]

State	Total				Mining and logging				Construction			
	December		January		December		January		December		January	
	2013	2014	2014	2015ᵖ	2013	2014	2014	2015ᵖ	2013	2014	2014	2015ᵖ
Alabama	1,923.7	1,948.2	1,885.4	1,922.8	11.9	11.6	11.8	11.2	79.3	80.0	76.2	77.1
Alaska	321.4	324.9	318.2	323.2	17.1	17.5	16.8	17.3	15.1	16.3	14.0	15.2
Arizona	2,592.5	2,643.8	2,536.5	2,602.8	13.0	13.1	13.0	12.9	125.9	126.0	123.7	126.0
Arkansas	1,182.7	1,208.4	1,160.9	1,190.4	9.0	8.9	8.7	8.6	44.3	47.5	43.9	47.2
California	15,546.6	15,994.3	15,280.1	15,768.5	30.3	30.8	30.1	30.0	651.8	681.8	637.9	679.2
Colorado	2,435.0	2,511.8	2,391.2	2,463.9	31.8	35.5	31.8	35.6	134.0	146.6	130.0	142.0
Connecticut	1,673.0	1,699.7	1,631.2	1,656.9	0.6	0.6	0.5	0.5	53.8	54.7	48.9	51.2
Delaware[1]	437.1	446.2	424.7	432.7	–	–	–	–	19.6	20.4	18.9	19.0
District of Columbia[1]	756.7	764.0	739.2	753.4	–	–	–	–	14.0	14.1	13.8	13.9
Florida	7,781.8	8,049.4	7,663.4	7,948.4	5.8	5.8	5.6	5.7	381.4	413.1	373.7	407.1
Georgia	4,106.6	4,249.2	4,041.4	4,183.5	9.0	8.9	9.0	8.9	149.3	157.3	147.4	151.6
Hawaii[1]	634.5	635.2	618.9	624.9	–	–	–	–	31.7	31.1	30.6	31.2
Idaho	646.2	659.2	631.2	649.3	3.9	3.7	3.8	3.5	33.6	37.0	31.7	34.8
Illinois	5,880.2	5,951.3	5,711.1	5,782.1	9.6	10.2	9.4	9.4	189.8	201.1	168.8	180.3
Indiana	2,997.6	3,033.3	2,885.8	2,957.7	7.1	7.1	6.7	6.7	120.9	120.4	108.2	107.6
Iowa	1,547.6	1,564.8	1,503.9	1,528.1	2.3	2.2	1.8	1.8	67.9	73.9	59.9	65.6
Kansas	1,395.9	1,412.0	1,359.6	1,378.6	10.8	10.6	10.4	10.1	57.9	58.9	55.3	56.1
Kentucky	1,864.4	1,892.9	1,811.3	1,851.8	16.9	16.0	16.2	15.7	69.4	73.7	64.1	69.3
Louisiana	1,975.6	2,010.2	1,946.2	1,970.6	53.8	52.5	53.9	51.5	129.7	139.8	129.7	133.3
Maine	603.3	604.5	580.3	581.3	2.6	2.5	2.6	2.5	25.3	25.1	22.7	22.5
Maryland[1]	2,623.8	2,655.8	2,543.4	2,582.8	–	–	–	–	147.4	153.5	142.3	148.3
Massachusetts	3,407.3	3,462.8	3,306.4	3,373.2	1.0	1.0	0.9	0.9	123.2	126.8	114.8	115.8
Michigan	4,169.3	4,237.5	4,065.0	4,155.6	8.0	8.3	7.8	8.0	133.0	139.0	122.8	131.3
Minnesota	2,807.6	2,829.6	2,733.3	2,769.3	6.9	6.9	6.6	6.7	98.1	97.8	87.9	87.8
Mississippi	1,123.1	1,129.3	1,107.4	1,120.6	9.1	9.3	9.1	8.9	50.5	46.3	48.8	44.2
Missouri	2,738.1	2,760.1	2,659.5	2,704.3	3.9	4.0	3.6	3.8	107.2	108.4	100.7	101.6
Montana	452.1	452.6	438.9	442.1	9.4	9.2	8.9	8.9	23.2	23.8	20.8	21.0
Nebraska[1]	994.8	1,000.2	971.1	982.7	–	–	–	–	44.3	45.2	41.5	41.6
Nevada	1,195.3	1,240.3	1,180.4	1,221.7	14.7	14.2	14.4	14.0	58.6	64.5	58.1	62.7
New Hampshire	651.5	657.5	632.5	640.8	1.0	0.9	0.9	0.9	22.7	23.9	20.8	21.9
New Jersey	3,988.9	4,014.3	3,860.9	3,906.8	1.4	1.4	1.3	1.3	137.6	147.0	127.6	138.2
New Mexico	821.4	833.2	806.5	816.7	26.6	28.4	26.8	28.2	42.4	43.3	41.7	41.6
New York	9,144.4	9,242.8	8,810.9	8,967.7	5.0	5.0	4.4	4.3	327.5	339.3	304.1	317.2
North Carolina	4,130.4	4,236.2	4,039.6	4,150.3	5.6	5.5	5.4	5.4	175.5	187.1	169.7	180.5
North Dakota	452.3	471.9	440.3	460.1	27.4	32.0	27.5	31.3	31.1	34.5	27.2	31.6
Ohio	5,341.1	5,388.6	5,180.4	5,276.2	13.3	15.4	13.1	14.9	185.1	186.5	169.1	169.7
Oklahoma	1,654.3	1,679.6	1,622.7	1,650.3	60.3	63.3	59.3	61.8	76.3	76.6	73.5	75.2
Oregon	1,701.3	1,754.7	1,669.1	1,728.1	7.5	7.4	7.4	7.1	75.4	78.2	74.1	76.6
Pennsylvania	5,804.4	5,869.8	5,652.2	5,719.9	36.0	37.2	35.4	37.4	215.6	229.0	203.3	212.8
Rhode Island	477.1	480.8	460.8	467.8	0.2	0.2	0.1	0.2	16.2	16.5	14.4	14.8
South Carolina	1,933.3	1,975.9	1,891.7	1,945.9	3.9	3.9	3.8	3.8	81.5	83.8	79.8	82.4
South Dakota[1]	420.0	422.6	410.1	412.9	–	–	–	–	20.9	21.3	18.8	19.3
Tennessee[1]	2,824.8	2,878.4	2,749.1	2,818.1	–	–	–	–	108.0	115.2	103.7	110.1
Texas	11,427.8	11,811.7	11,235.4	11,632.3	292.2	317.3	293.1	314.0	619.7	668.1	614.6	664.5
Utah	1,323.4	1,365.2	1,293.8	1,347.4	12.1	12.4	11.9	11.9	74.1	79.6	70.9	77.2
Vermont	315.1	319.1	306.7	311.9	0.8	0.8	0.7	0.7	14.2	14.4	12.7	13.1
Virginia	3,785.4	3,817.2	3,706.0	3,739.3	9.9	9.1	9.7	8.9	175.5	176.8	169.4	174.8
Washington	3,035.3	3,127.4	2,997.7	3,098.6	6.2	6.1	6.0	5.9	149.8	163.3	146.8	163.8
West Virginia	772.5	767.3	744.9	746.5	31.1	30.5	30.1	30.2	32.5	30.8	29.1	27.7
Wisconsin	2,845.1	2,881.6	2,759.4	2,810.6	3.6	4.1	3.4	3.9	96.1	103.9	87.1	93.8
Wyoming	288.3	292.3	281.6	286.8	27.0	27.5	26.9	26.4	21.6	22.4	20.2	20.9
Puerto Rico[1]	960.0	928.6	908.7	902.5	–	–	–	–	32.1	28.8	26.8	26.0
Virgin Islands[1]	38.5	38.3	37.6	38.0	–	–	–	–	1.4	1.6	1.3	1.6

[1] Mining and logging is combined with construction.

p Preliminary

NOTE: Data are counts of jobs by place of work. Data have been revised to reflect 2014 benchmarks. Unadjusted data from April 2013 are subject to revision. Estimates subsequent to the current benchmark month are preliminary and will be revised when new information becomes available.

Table 6. Employees on nonfarm payrolls by state and selected industry sector, not seasonally adjusted- Continued

[In thousands]

State	Manufacturing				Trade, transportation, and utilities				Information			
	December		January		December		January		December		January	
	2013	2014	2014	2015ᵖ	2013	2014	2014	2015ᵖ	2013	2014	2014	2015ᵖ
Alabama	252.0	254.1	250.5	252.2	381.6	385.5	367.3	373.9	22.9	21.9	22.2	22.3
Alaska	7.9	6.9	12.2	10.8	62.5	64.2	60.2	63.0	6.3	6.2	6.2	6.2
Arizona	155.8	156.3	155.7	154.9	506.7	517.1	488.7	500.3	42.4	43.1	42.3	42.3
Arkansas	152.7	157.4	152.4	155.0	246.7	252.9	239.2	246.9	14.1	13.5	13.8	13.5
California	1,261.0	1,264.6	1,249.0	1,254.7	2,933.8	3,011.4	2,824.7	2,910.2	459.5	467.7	452.8	461.8
Colorado	134.0	138.9	133.1	137.2	437.8	445.4	424.1	434.8	70.1	69.6	70.1	68.6
Connecticut	161.4	159.6	160.4	158.4	312.1	317.0	299.0	300.7	32.2	31.4	31.9	31.0
Delaware	25.5	25.8	25.2	25.6	82.3	83.1	77.7	79.2	5.0	4.8	5.1	4.8
District of Columbia	1.0	1.0	1.0	1.0	30.7	33.2	29.5	31.8	16.7	17.0	17.1	17.0
Florida	327.9	332.8	326.8	329.1	1,652.4	1,697.5	1,597.2	1,657.8	135.9	137.1	135.6	134.7
Georgia	360.8	371.4	360.1	372.4	877.6	912.4	852.8	889.5	105.3	109.2	104.7	105.8
Hawaii	13.8	13.6	13.5	13.4	121.1	121.5	117.1	119.5	9.9	8.7	8.3	8.2
Idaho	59.9	59.4	59.3	59.7	132.5	134.9	128.6	130.4	9.3	9.4	9.1	9.3
Illinois	579.0	582.7	574.4	574.5	1,203.4	1,217.6	1,156.0	1,168.7	98.6	99.4	97.3	98.6
Indiana	498.3	514.6	495.5	512.2	589.0	594.7	562.7	578.8	35.8	35.3	35.3	35.7
Iowa	216.2	215.8	214.6	214.9	318.9	322.1	307.3	314.0	25.8	25.2	25.8	25.0
Kansas	162.0	162.7	159.7	158.0	268.3	270.3	259.2	266.6	28.1	28.1	28.0	28.2
Kentucky	232.9	237.6	230.9	238.4	385.4	391.3	368.9	378.5	26.2	26.2	26.4	25.7
Louisiana	146.4	149.9	146.3	148.8	395.5	403.4	383.2	391.4	25.7	26.5	23.6	26.1
Maine	50.5	51.1	48.6	48.9	123.4	123.5	115.8	116.1	7.5	7.3	7.5	7.3
Maryland	104.4	102.7	103.0	101.4	471.1	473.6	449.4	453.8	38.8	37.2	39.1	37.0
Massachusetts	251.7	248.9	249.5	247.5	576.1	583.3	555.8	564.6	86.1	87.0	84.6	87.0
Michigan	565.0	588.5	558.3	584.3	771.3	778.3	740.0	755.0	56.1	57.0	56.3	57.0
Minnesota	308.0	314.8	305.1	310.8	527.2	531.7	506.8	514.4	53.1	53.7	52.6	52.3
Mississippi	139.1	140.0	139.0	139.8	225.3	227.0	217.2	223.9	13.2	13.2	13.8	13.3
Missouri	252.7	260.9	248.4	258.8	534.8	536.5	513.5	519.3	57.4	57.2	56.5	57.3
Montana	19.1	19.1	18.4	18.4	94.3	95.7	90.8	93.4	6.7	6.6	6.5	6.5
Nebraska	97.3	97.0	96.6	96.4	209.6	207.5	201.2	200.8	17.2	17.1	17.2	17.2
Nevada	41.2	42.0	41.2	41.5	233.5	240.9	224.9	234.0	13.1	13.6	12.7	13.4
New Hampshire	66.6	67.0	66.1	66.8	141.7	143.9	135.7	138.6	11.9	11.8	12.0	11.8
New Jersey	244.9	243.7	241.3	241.7	860.7	872.9	824.4	843.3	75.2	75.1	74.4	73.7
New Mexico	28.5	28.3	28.0	27.8	141.1	142.7	136.5	138.9	12.3	12.7	11.6	12.2
New York	457.5	451.5	449.1	443.7	1,605.4	1,622.3	1,533.1	1,559.2	267.9	265.2	260.0	262.5
North Carolina	446.2	457.3	441.6	456.3	789.5	807.7	759.4	777.4	71.9	74.0	71.0	73.5
North Dakota	25.6	26.5	25.2	25.9	105.3	108.9	102.7	106.9	6.8	6.7	6.8	6.7
Ohio	669.7	677.0	662.7	676.1	1,022.5	1,025.4	975.2	998.1	74.7	72.0	73.0	71.5
Oklahoma	137.2	139.1	136.3	139.1	305.9	309.2	296.7	300.6	21.9	21.5	21.7	21.6
Oregon	175.1	180.9	174.1	180.2	329.8	340.1	318.0	330.9	32.7	33.0	31.7	32.4
Pennsylvania	566.2	571.1	561.5	567.8	1,140.4	1,163.3	1,096.2	1,114.9	87.1	85.8	85.0	85.2
Rhode Island	40.8	41.8	40.3	41.1	77.2	77.3	73.5	75.0	9.0	8.8	9.0	8.7
South Carolina	227.2	234.0	226.3	231.2	377.0	386.2	363.4	376.9	26.4	27.0	26.0	26.6
South Dakota	41.3	43.2	41.1	42.6	85.8	86.6	83.5	85.1	6.0	6.1	6.0	6.0
Tennessee	322.6	330.7	321.0	330.0	605.0	613.2	579.2	596.2	44.3	44.5	43.6	44.2
Texas	879.0	893.2	870.1	884.8	2,335.1	2,406.4	2,265.9	2,343.9	204.9	205.1	201.7	206.0
Utah	120.0	121.4	119.1	121.9	257.0	267.6	246.6	259.1	33.4	33.8	32.6	34.1
Vermont	31.9	31.2	30.9	30.1	57.7	58.3	54.9	55.9	4.8	4.6	4.8	4.6
Virginia	232.0	233.5	229.6	231.9	667.6	671.6	636.0	644.0	71.4	70.9	72.2	69.9
Washington	285.5	289.1	283.5	287.1	574.7	594.4	555.6	576.8	107.4	109.6	107.0	109.5
West Virginia	48.4	47.6	47.7	47.4	141.1	139.1	133.8	134.4	9.8	9.6	9.6	9.5
Wisconsin	458.3	467.9	455.7	468.5	537.0	543.1	513.4	521.8	47.9	48.7	47.4	49.3
Wyoming	9.9	10.1	9.6	9.8	55.1	56.1	53.4	55.4	3.8	3.8	3.8	3.8
Puerto Rico	78.4	75.6	74.8	73.7	190.1	184.3	178.0	179.0	20.0	20.4	20.8	20.0
Virgin Islands	0.7	0.6	0.6	0.6	8.5	8.2	8.3	8.2	0.8	0.8	0.7	0.8

p Preliminary

NOTE: Data are counts of jobs by place of work. Data have been revised to reflect 2014 benchmarks. Unadjusted data from April 2013 are subject to revision. Estimates subsequent to the current benchmark month are preliminary and will be revised when new information becomes available.

Table 6. Employees on nonfarm payrolls by state and selected industry sector, not seasonally adjusted-Continued

[In thousands]

State	Financial activities				Professional and business services				Education and health services			
	December		January		December		January		December		January	
	2013	2014	2014	2015ᵖ	2013	2014	2014	2015ᵖ	2013	2014	2014	2015ᵖ
Alabama.	95.0	95.0	93.8	95.4	220.8	225.6	215.9	225.6	225.5	228.6	219.8	226.3
Alaska.	12.0	12.4	11.9	12.0	29.5	28.4	28.7	28.1	47.1	47.5	46.5	47.1
Arizona.	190.1	192.7	187.1	191.2	390.5	397.5	374.3	390.7	379.7	394.0	374.9	391.9
Arkansas.	49.9	49.8	49.1	49.4	130.7	133.8	128.0	133.4	172.9	174.4	170.7	173.3
California.	785.0	794.0	775.3	794.4	2,400.4	2,503.6	2,354.4	2,467.2	2,388.8	2,465.8	2,363.5	2,441.8
Colorado.	153.4	156.6	151.5	155.0	378.5	389.7	370.1	376.9	293.5	306.2	291.2	305.9
Connecticut.	129.3	128.7	128.2	128.6	209.4	215.9	203.1	209.4	325.0	333.0	320.4	328.7
Delaware.	44.5	46.4	44.1	46.3	60.5	63.0	57.9	60.7	71.9	73.5	71.4	72.5
District of Columbia.	29.8	30.6	29.7	30.4	156.6	160.9	153.7	159.0	131.2	131.3	127.4	126.7
Florida.	521.0	534.8	512.6	527.1	1,148.7	1,201.6	1,127.8	1,183.3	1,145.6	1,191.1	1,134.4	1,182.5
Georgia.	230.8	236.5	229.2	236.5	600.8	631.5	591.5	613.7	518.4	535.6	513.3	533.4
Hawaii.	27.5	27.8	27.1	27.3	82.1	84.0	81.2	83.4	79.7	80.2	78.0	78.6
Idaho.	31.9	33.3	31.8	33.5	79.7	78.4	76.2	78.5	93.1	94.6	92.8	95.0
Illinois.	370.6	369.4	366.5	366.0	914.3	927.5	878.8	896.7	887.6	901.6	875.6	890.0
Indiana.	128.8	131.0	126.2	129.5	322.2	329.2	304.5	316.2	444.1	446.1	433.7	440.0
Iowa.	104.5	104.8	103.5	104.1	134.8	135.9	131.2	135.1	226.1	229.1	220.3	223.0
Kansas.	79.4	79.7	78.5	80.0	168.3	173.2	163.5	168.0	189.0	192.4	187.1	188.8
Kentucky.	89.6	90.5	88.8	89.5	215.6	221.6	204.1	211.4	261.9	265.2	258.6	263.3
Louisiana.	92.1	93.2	91.0	93.6	211.8	214.0	209.2	208.3	297.7	302.8	296.3	302.6
Maine.	30.4	30.4	29.9	29.9	61.9	62.8	59.9	60.9	122.7	124.3	121.7	121.3
Maryland.	145.3	144.2	143.1	143.1	418.7	426.0	408.9	420.4	429.0	438.9	419.8	432.2
Massachusetts.	207.4	209.4	204.9	208.2	511.8	521.9	497.6	510.3	736.7	751.9	717.2	737.1
Michigan.	202.9	206.0	202.3	203.8	613.5	633.7	597.8	627.6	648.0	654.6	636.5	644.4
Minnesota.	178.7	178.6	177.0	178.0	353.7	357.4	341.6	349.7	497.5	504.8	491.8	500.3
Mississippi.	43.9	44.5	43.2	43.9	101.1	103.1	99.6	103.6	135.1	137.8	133.7	136.9
Missouri.	164.2	165.1	162.2	164.4	352.9	357.9	340.7	349.8	435.2	437.9	429.7	433.9
Montana.	24.6	26.0	24.1	25.6	38.9	39.0	37.5	38.3	70.3	70.2	69.7	69.2
Nebraska.	72.1	73.0	71.9	72.5	113.2	112.1	110.0	111.3	148.2	151.5	145.7	150.5
Nevada.	57.6	57.4	56.5	56.5	151.4	159.2	152.9	159.2	113.8	119.6	113.0	118.3
New Hampshire.	35.8	35.7	35.3	35.6	72.2	73.4	71.0	71.7	116.0	117.6	114.3	116.6
New Jersey.	249.9	246.9	245.4	244.7	640.5	635.7	615.4	609.0	639.7	645.6	626.8	639.2
New Mexico.	33.8	33.6	33.1	33.4	99.0	100.3	98.1	99.8	126.5	131.9	126.1	130.8
New York.	690.9	692.6	680.8	688.8	1,223.8	1,245.1	1,183.5	1,209.1	1,870.1	1,903.1	1,803.9	1,860.4
North Carolina.	207.9	212.2	206.9	211.4	556.7	587.4	544.9	577.2	565.3	578.7	557.8	569.8
North Dakota.	23.6	24.2	23.5	24.2	34.2	35.8	33.8	35.4	59.6	60.0	59.0	59.1
Ohio.	286.3	289.8	283.7	288.9	706.4	716.5	683.4	700.8	893.8	898.2	878.8	891.8
Oklahoma.	79.6	79.9	78.6	79.5	181.8	192.0	179.0	188.6	228.4	231.0	226.2	230.1
Oregon.	91.9	92.7	90.3	91.8	213.5	223.5	208.7	221.6	247.5	256.8	243.5	253.2
Pennsylvania.	315.1	313.7	312.5	313.6	753.8	761.0	734.5	746.3	1,182.6	1,201.2	1,160.2	1,175.8
Rhode Island.	32.4	32.4	32.1	32.4	59.7	60.5	57.0	58.8	105.8	106.7	103.4	103.3
South Carolina.	96.1	97.0	94.6	96.7	251.7	260.0	242.9	253.4	223.7	229.4	221.8	226.7
South Dakota.	30.1	29.5	29.6	29.3	30.2	29.5	29.5	29.3	68.6	69.3	67.7	68.5
Tennessee.	140.1	142.4	138.9	142.3	375.8	388.1	359.5	374.7	402.4	409.1	397.5	404.3
Texas.	694.1	714.8	686.8	706.9	1,512.3	1,577.2	1,483.8	1,554.5	1,510.6	1,560.9	1,491.1	1,546.7
Utah.	74.8	77.6	73.2	77.0	184.9	191.3	178.8	189.0	175.5	179.8	173.2	179.2
Vermont.	12.1	12.3	12.0	12.3	26.3	26.4	25.2	25.5	62.5	63.6	61.9	62.8
Virginia.	193.9	193.4	190.8	193.4	674.0	678.3	665.4	664.4	492.5	503.8	494.1	500.8
Washington.	151.9	156.8	150.7	156.8	365.3	378.6	358.8	376.0	449.4	463.2	446.7	459.7
West Virginia.	31.3	31.2	30.9	30.4	64.5	68.4	63.6	67.1	128.2	127.9	124.9	126.4
Wisconsin.	150.4	154.2	147.9	152.7	307.7	306.4	298.0	297.5	431.0	435.1	422.8	429.2
Wyoming.	11.2	11.4	11.0	11.4	17.7	18.4	17.1	18.3	27.1	27.5	27.0	27.6
Puerto Rico.	44.4	42.7	43.4	42.3	123.9	116.0	113.8	111.9	130.0	128.3	119.1	123.2
Virgin Islands.	2.2	2.2	2.2	2.2	3.4	3.4	3.3	3.4	2.4	2.4	2.3	2.4

p Preliminary

NOTE: Data are counts of jobs by place of work. Data have been revised to reflect 2014 benchmarks. Unadjusted data from April 2013 are subject to revision. Estimates subsequent to the current benchmark month are preliminary and will be revised when new information becomes available.

Table 6. Employees on nonfarm payrolls by state and selected industry sector, not seasonally adjusted-
Continued

[In thousands]

State	Leisure and hospitality				Other services				Government			
	December		January		December		January		December		January	
	2013	2014	2014	2015ᵖ	2013	2014	2014	2015ᵖ	2013	2014	2014	2015ᵖ
Alabama	176.8	183.5	173.1	180.0	79.2	80.4	78.7	80.6	378.7	382.0	376.1	378.2
Alaska	29.5	30.6	28.8	29.9	11.5	11.6	11.5	11.7	82.9	83.3	81.4	81.9
Arizona	280.8	290.6	277.0	290.3	87.5	91.2	86.1	92.7	420.1	422.2	413.7	409.6
Arkansas	102.3	108.9	101.1	107.8	43.0	43.9	42.8	44.0	217.1	217.4	211.2	211.3
California	1,706.9	1,776.9	1,678.1	1,750.1	522.9	544.8	521.4	539.9	2,406.2	2,452.9	2,392.9	2,439.2
Colorado	292.4	307.1	291.7	308.2	98.0	100.4	98.5	99.5	411.5	415.8	399.1	400.2
Connecticut	146.2	151.7	140.2	147.0	62.1	63.4	61.5	62.3	240.9	243.7	237.1	239.1
Delaware	43.7	44.6	41.7	42.8	18.5	18.1	18.2	17.8	65.6	66.5	64.5	64.0
District of Columbia	67.5	69.3	65.4	67.4	69.5	70.0	69.0	70.6	239.7	236.6	232.6	235.6
Florida	1,054.2	1,107.2	1,047.5	1,097.2	316.5	332.1	317.0	330.8	1,092.4	1,096.3	1,085.2	1,093.1
Georgia	412.0	437.9	403.6	429.4	151.6	155.9	150.7	154.6	691.0	692.6	679.1	687.7
Hawaii	113.2	114.3	112.0	113.8	26.8	26.1	26.4	25.9	128.7	127.9	124.7	123.6
Idaho	61.9	64.2	61.0	64.0	21.9	22.8	21.7	22.9	118.5	121.5	115.2	117.7
Illinois	538.0	548.5	524.1	532.5	250.3	251.4	247.5	249.2	839.0	841.9	812.7	816.2
Indiana	286.8	287.9	273.8	277.4	124.2	125.3	122.3	125.1	440.4	441.7	416.9	428.5
Iowa	132.2	133.3	128.8	130.2	58.6	58.7	58.2	58.0	260.3	263.8	252.5	256.4
Kansas	119.6	122.5	115.6	120.1	49.0	50.2	47.9	48.6	263.5	263.4	254.4	254.1
Kentucky	176.1	179.8	169.8	175.4	63.9	63.3	62.8	62.9	326.5	327.7	320.7	321.7
Louisiana	214.3	223.7	212.4	219.4	70.9	72.5	70.9	71.8	337.7	331.9	329.7	323.8
Maine	55.3	53.9	51.7	51.7	20.6	20.8	20.4	20.7	103.1	102.8	99.5	99.5
Maryland	247.1	252.9	237.0	242.0	111.6	113.2	109.9	111.3	510.4	513.6	490.9	493.3
Massachusetts	325.3	329.6	310.0	314.7	129.5	133.7	127.1	132.5	458.5	469.3	444.0	454.6
Michigan	390.9	391.8	377.8	384.2	170.0	171.0	168.3	168.6	610.6	609.3	597.1	591.4
Minnesota	243.0	245.1	236.7	240.8	113.3	115.2	111.1	113.3	428.1	423.6	416.1	415.2
Mississippi	123.4	124.2	121.2	122.2	38.7	38.7	38.5	39.3	243.7	245.2	243.3	244.6
Missouri	273.7	277.6	262.2	269.4	112.4	113.6	111.2	113.7	443.7	441.0	430.8	432.3
Montana	57.9	56.9	56.8	56.1	17.9	17.4	17.4	17.4	89.8	88.7	88.0	87.3
Nebraska	84.9	85.7	82.7	84.0	36.5	37.3	36.2	38.2	171.5	173.8	168.1	170.2
Nevada	322.4	339.5	322.2	338.8	33.6	33.9	33.5	34.1	155.4	155.5	151.0	149.2
New Hampshire	62.8	62.6	61.5	62.2	25.4	25.8	25.3	26.0	95.4	94.9	89.6	88.7
New Jersey	342.3	340.9	325.7	327.7	166.1	169.9	163.5	168.0	630.6	635.2	615.1	620.0
New Mexico	88.6	89.0	87.7	87.1	27.5	28.3	27.3	28.5	195.1	194.7	189.6	188.4
New York	844.7	858.9	799.4	811.8	392.5	399.2	385.2	397.3	1,459.1	1,460.6	1,407.4	1,413.4
North Carolina	429.0	441.7	414.3	427.1	147.2	152.2	145.7	150.8	735.6	732.4	722.9	720.9
North Dakota	39.6	41.9	38.2	40.2	16.4	17.8	16.4	17.7	82.7	83.6	80.0	81.1
Ohio	506.9	524.4	485.8	510.2	208.5	208.8	205.8	208.0	773.9	774.6	749.8	746.2
Oklahoma	150.1	152.3	148.4	149.6	58.9	59.3	58.4	58.9	353.9	355.4	344.6	345.3
Oregon	174.2	179.1	171.3	175.9	57.6	60.0	57.4	59.2	296.1	303.0	292.6	299.2
Pennsylvania	522.6	525.4	501.8	509.7	251.4	255.6	249.1	251.7	733.6	726.5	712.7	704.7
Rhode Island	51.9	52.6	48.4	50.0	22.6	22.9	22.0	23.0	61.3	61.1	60.6	60.5
South Carolina	216.7	219.0	209.7	217.8	71.0	71.6	70.2	72.0	358.1	364.0	353.2	358.4
South Dakota	42.9	42.2	41.3	39.9	15.7	16.0	15.6	15.7	78.5	78.9	77.0	77.2
Tennessee	284.9	294.9	276.0	286.0	104.9	104.8	104.2	103.2	436.8	435.5	425.5	427.1
Texas	1,139.3	1,194.3	1,119.0	1,173.1	399.4	409.8	398.5	407.4	1,841.2	1,864.6	1,810.8	1,830.5
Utah	125.2	131.0	123.6	129.6	36.4	37.5	36.3	37.4	230.0	233.2	227.6	231.0
Vermont	36.5	38.4	37.2	39.6	10.1	10.3	9.9	10.1	58.2	58.8	56.5	57.2
Virginia	358.9	364.9	345.1	351.2	193.9	195.9	191.8	195.0	715.8	719.0	701.9	705.0
Washington	287.1	290.8	282.2	288.2	111.6	116.6	111.0	114.5	546.4	558.9	549.4	560.3
West Virginia	73.6	71.1	70.5	69.2	55.4	54.8	54.8	54.8	156.6	156.3	149.9	149.4
Wisconsin	252.6	256.7	242.5	248.6	138.3	139.7	136.0	138.2	422.2	421.8	405.2	407.1
Wyoming	32.5	33.1	32.1	33.0	10.0	9.8	9.9	9.6	72.4	72.2	70.6	70.6
Puerto Rico	81.8	81.4	79.4	79.9	18.5	17.9	17.5	17.1	240.8	233.2	235.1	229.4
Virgin Islands	7.2	7.4	7.4	7.4	1.0	0.8	1.0	0.8	10.9	10.9	10.5	10.6

p Preliminary
NOTE: Data are counts of jobs by place of work. Data have been revised to reflect 2014 benchmarks. Unadjusted data from April 2013 are subject to revision. Estimates subsequent to the current benchmark month are preliminary and will be revised when new information becomes available.

Chart 1. Unemployment rates by state, seasonally adjusted January 2015

(U.S. rate = 5.7 percent)

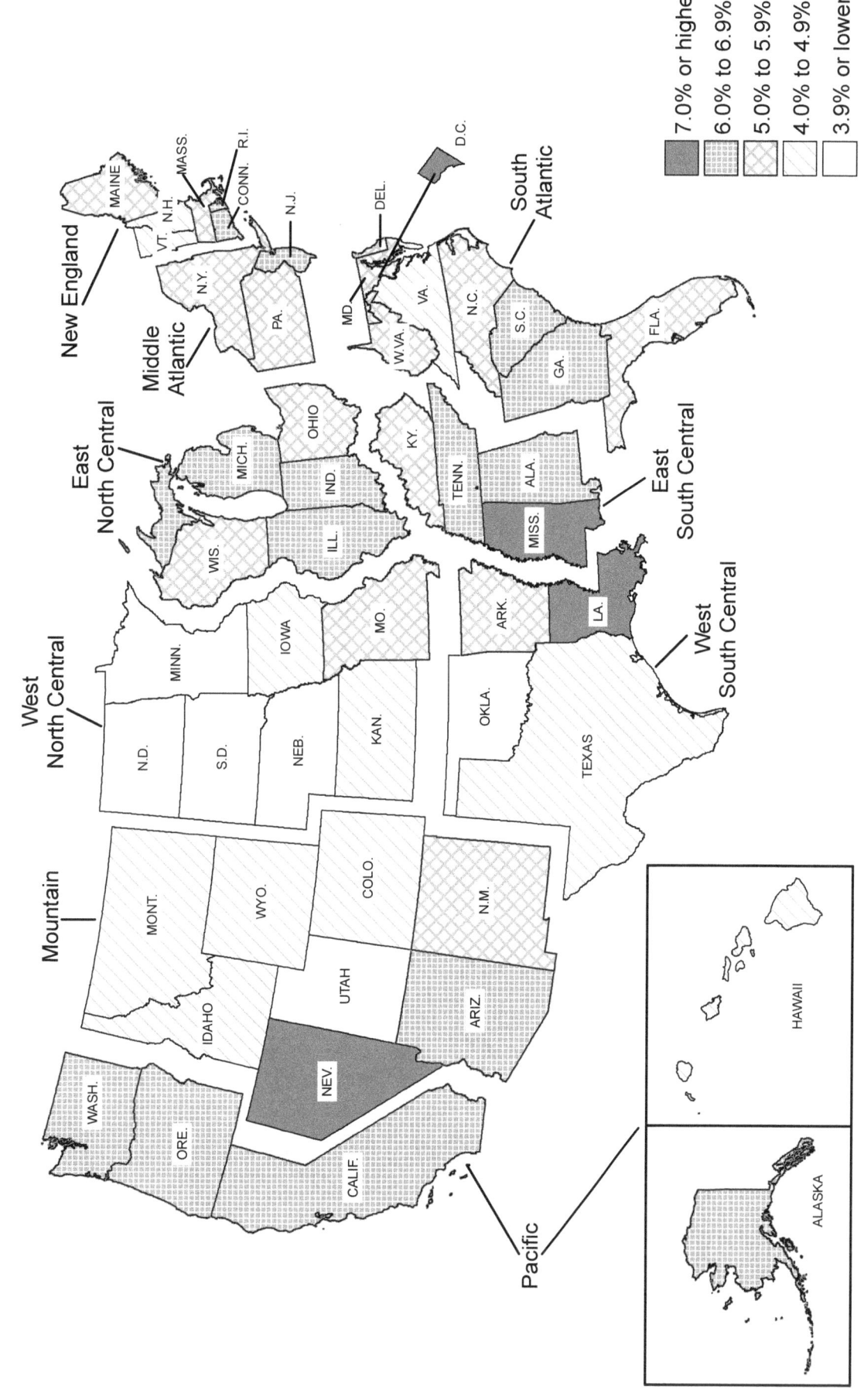

Legend:
- 7.0% or higher
- 6.0% to 6.9%
- 5.0% to 5.9%
- 4.0% to 4.9%
- 3.9% or lower

Chart 2. Percentage change in nonfarm employment by state, seasonally adjusted, January 2014–January 2015

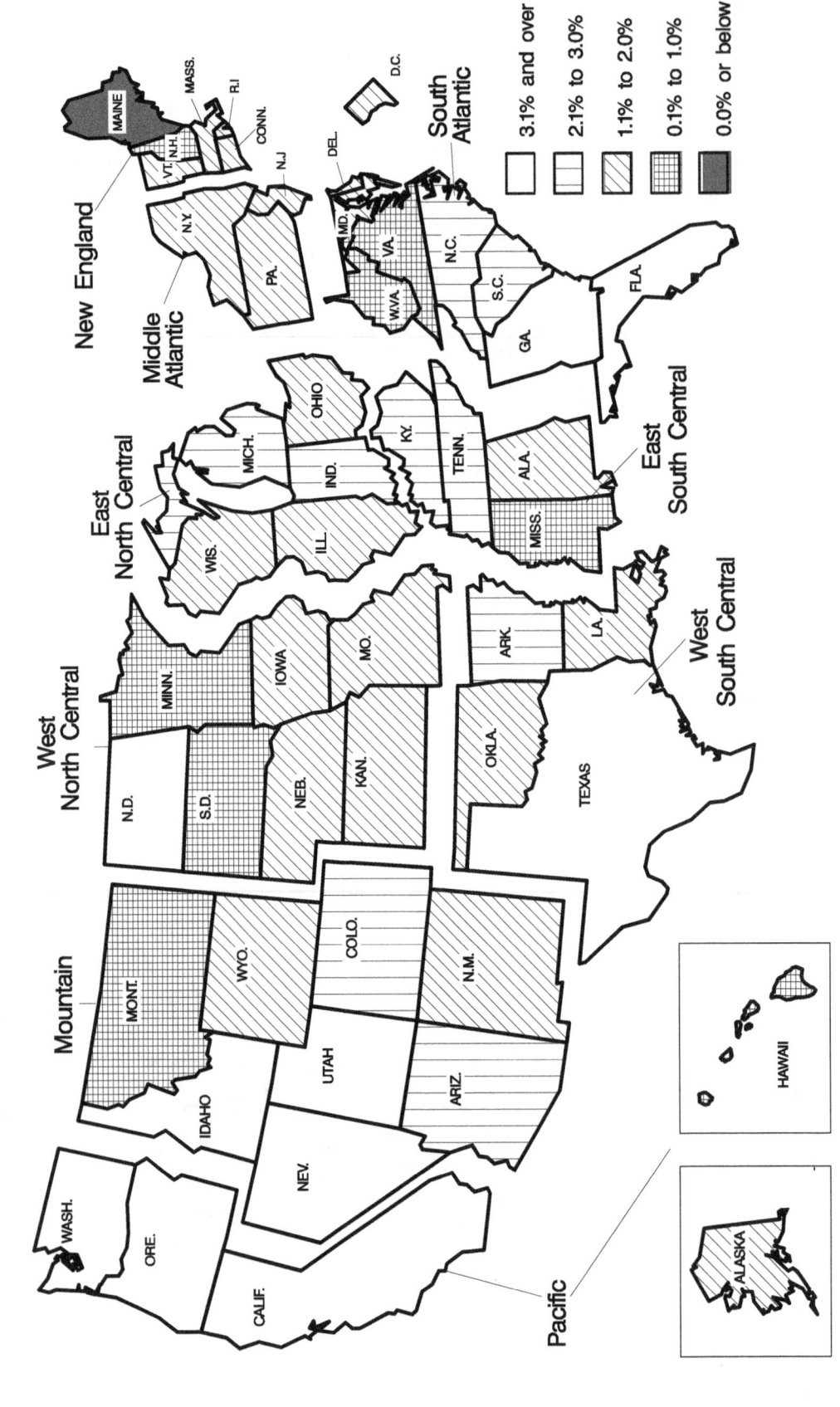

Legend:
- 3.1% and over
- 2.1% to 3.0%
- 1.1% to 2.0%
- 0.1% to 1.0%
- 0.0% or below